COOKING FOR CHRISTMAS

COOKING FOR CHRISTMAS

Grange BOOKS

Published by Grange Books
An imprint of Books & Toys Limited
The Grange
Grange Yard
London SE1 3AG
By arrangement with Ebury Press

ISBN 1 85627 191 9

Consultant editor: Jeni Wright
Editors: Veronica Sperling and Barbara Croxford
Design: Mike Leaman
Illustrations: John Woodcock and Kate Simunek
Photography: David Johnson
Cookery: Susanna Tee, Maxine Clark, Janet Smith

Filmset by Advanced Filmsetters (Glasgow) Ltd

Printed and bound in Italy by
New Interlitho, S.p.a., Milan

CONTENTS

COOKERY NOTES

Follow either metric or imperial measures for the recipes in this book as they are not inter-changeable. Sets of spoon measures are available in both metric and imperial size to give accurate measurement of small quantities. All spoon measures are level unless otherwise stated. When measuring milk we have used the exact conversion of 568 ml (1 pint).
* Size 4 eggs should be used except when otherwise stated.
† Granulated sugar is used unless otherwise stated.
● Plain flour is used unless otherwise stated.

OVEN TEMPERATURE CHART

°C	°F	Gas mark
110	225	$\frac{1}{4}$
130	250	$\frac{1}{2}$
140	275	1
150	300	2
170	325	3
180	350	4
190	375	5
200	400	6
220	425	7
230	450	8
240	475	9

KEY TO SYMBOLS

$\boxed{1.00^*}$ Indicates minimum preparation and cooking times in hours and minutes. They do not include prepared items in the list of ingredients; calculated times apply only to the method. An asterisk * indicates extra time should be allowed, so check the note below symbols.

⌂ Chef's hats indicate degree of difficulty of a recipe: no hat means it is straightforward; one hat slightly more complicated; two hats indicates that it is for more advanced cooks.

£ Indicates a recipe which is good value for money; £ £ indicates an expensive recipe. No £ sign indicates an inexpensive recipe.

✳ Indicates that a recipe will freeze. If there is no symbol, the recipe is unsuitable for freezing. An asterisk * indicates special freezer instructions so check the note immediately below the symbols.

$\boxed{309 \text{ cals}}$ Indicates calories per serving, including any suggestions (e.g. cream, to serve) given in the ingredients.

METRIC CONVERSION SCALE

LIQUID				SOLID		
Imperial	Exact conversion	Recommended ml		Imperial	Exact conversion	Recommended g
$\frac{1}{4}$ pint	142 ml	150 ml		1 oz	28.35 g	25 g
$\frac{1}{2}$ pint	284 ml	300 ml		2 oz	56.7 g	50 g
1 pint	568 ml	600 ml		4 oz	113.4 g	100 g
$1\frac{1}{2}$ pints	851 ml	900 ml		8 oz	226.8 g	225 g
$1\frac{3}{4}$ pints	992 ml	1 litre		12 oz	340.2 g	350 g
For quantities of $1\frac{3}{4}$ pints and over,				14 oz	397.0 g	400 g
litres and fractions of a litre have				16 oz (1 lb)	453.6 g	450 g
been used.				1 kilogram (kg) equals 2.2 lb.		

COOKING FOR CHRISTMAS

Here in one volume is everything you need to know about cooking at Christmas time, from simple, light dishes for family meals, to sumptuous buffet party spreads. There are Christmas specialities from all over the world, traditional main courses, desserts and puddings, plus lots of baking recipes to help you entertain with confidence. And the special chapter on Food for Presents is full of ideas for making edible gifts, the most personal of all the Christmas presents you are likely to give. Every recipe is photographed in colour, and there are step-by-step illustrations to help with cooking methods.

In the tinted section at the back of the book you can read interesting facts about how other countries celebrate Christmas, advice and information on buying special ingredients for the festive season, and an invaluable countdown to Christmas which will guide you smoothly through the most hectic time of the year. There is additional information on preserving, wrapping and packaging, plus a foolproof guide to making the Christmas cake, and lots of basic recipes from vegetables, sauces and stuffings to imaginative leftovers and exciting party drinks.

Light Dishes

At Christmas, there are
lots of times when you
need to cook something
quick and light, often at
a moment's notice.
Traditional festive fare
has its place, but it's the
in-between meals that
can easily get forgotten.
This chapter helps bridge
the gap at Christmastime,
with a selection of
delicious light dishes to
help balance the diet.

CHINESE BEEF AND VEGETABLE STIR FRY

| 0.25* | £ £ | 389 cals |

* plus 1 hour marinating

Serves 4

350 g (12 oz) fillet or rump steak,
  sliced into very thin strips
  (see box)

30 ml (2 tbsp) cornflour

60 ml (4 tbsp) soy sauce

90 ml (6 tbsp) dry sherry

30 ml (2 tbsp) dark soft brown
  sugar

30 ml (2 tbsp) wine vinegar

salt and freshly ground pepper

75 ml (5 tbsp) sesame and
  vegetable oil (see box)

1 onion, skinned and thinly sliced

1 garlic clove, skinned and crushed

2.5 cm (1 inch) piece fresh root
  ginger, skinned and crushed

2 celery sticks, trimmed and thinly
  sliced

1 red pepper, cored, seeded and
  sliced into thin strips

225 g (8 oz) mange-touts, halved

1 Put the steak in a bowl. Mix
together the next 5 ingredients
with salt and pepper to taste. Pour
over the steak, stir well to mix,
then cover and leave to marinate
for 1 hour.

2 Heat 30 ml (2 tbsp) of the oil in
a wok or large frying pan. Add
the onion, garlic and ginger and
fry gently for 5 minutes until soft.

3 Heat another 15 ml (1 tbsp) of
the oil in the wok. Add the
celery and red pepper and fry,
stirring, for a further 5 minutes
until tender but still crisp.
Remove the vegetables from the
wok with a slotted spoon.

4 Drain the steak from the
marinade. Heat the remaining
oil in the wok, add the steak and
stir fry over high heat for 5
minutes. Remove with a slotted
spoon and set aside with the
vegetables.

5 Add the mange-touts to the
wok and stir fry over high heat
for 2–3 minutes. Return the steak
and vegetables to the wok, then
pour in the marinade and stir until
bubbling and well mixed. Taste
and season. You may not need any
salt as soy sauce is salty. Serve
immediately.

Menu Suggestion
Serve this colourful dish for a
quick family supper on a bed of
boiled Chinese noodles, which can
be cooked at the same time.

**CHINESE BEEF AND
VEGETABLE STIR FRY**
In Chinese cooking, especially
in stir-fried dishes when food
needs to be cooked really
quickly, cutting and slicing is
very important. One of the
easiest ways to cut meat as thinly
as possible is to freeze it first.
Simply put the whole piece of
steak in the freezer for about 4
hours, then slice it while it is
frozen—you will be amazed at
how thinly it can be sliced.
There is no need to wait for the
meat to defrost, by the time it
has been marinating for 1 hour,
it will be ready to cook.
  Sesame oil is available in
bottles from oriental specialist
shops, and some good supermarkets and delicatessens. It is
made from roasted sesame seeds,
and is very strong. For frying,
it is best to mix sesame oil with
vegetable oil, to dilute the
intense flavour.

HOME-MADE PÂTÉ DE FOIE

| 0.20* | 🍴 | £ £ | 275 cals |

* plus 1¼ hours chilling

Serves 6

450 g (1 lb) calf's or chicken's liver

100 g (4 oz) pork fat

1 small garlic clove, skinned

50 g (2 oz) cooked tongue, chopped into tiny cubes

salt and freshly ground pepper

15 g (½ oz) aspic powder

mushrooms and blanched green leek, to decorate

curly endive or radicchio, to garnish

1 Mince the liver and pork fat with the garlic.

2 Heat a heavy-based frying pan. When hot, add the liver mixture and stir well. When the liver has changed colour, add a very little water and allow to simmer for 5 minutes.

3 Press the mixture through a fine sieve or purée in a blender or food processor. Add the tongue. Taste and season.

4 Make up the aspic jelly with 300 ml (½ pint) water, using the packet instructions. Leave until on the point of setting.

5 Line the bases of 6 ramekins or 6 small soufflé dishes with a layer of aspic and a decoration cut from thin slices of mushroom or blanched leek. Leave to set in the refrigerator for 15 minutes.

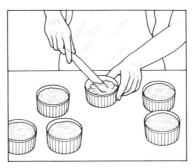

6 When the decoration has set, fill each dish with pâté, spread evenly, and chill in the refrigerator for at least 1 hour until firm.

7 To serve, dip each ramekin briefly in warm water and unmould. Garnish with a few endive or radicchio leaves.

Menu Suggestion

Pâté de Foie makes a tasty snack at any time of day. Serve with crisp Melba toast or crusty French bread and butter. A robust French red wine would complement the strong flavour of the pâté.

SMOKED HADDOCK GOUGÈRES

| 1.20 | 🍳 | £ | 605 cals |

Serves 4

90 g (3½ oz) butter

150 g (5 oz) plain flour

3 eggs, beaten

450 g (1 lb) smoked haddock

1 medium onion, skinned and
   chopped

300 ml (½ pint) milk

10 ml (2 tsp) capers

2 hard-boiled eggs, shelled and
   chopped

2 tomatoes, skinned, seeded and
   cut into strips

salt and freshly ground pepper

lemon juice, to taste

15 ml (1 tbsp) fresh white
   breadcrumbs

15 g (½ oz) Cheddar, grated

chopped fresh parsley, to garnish
   (optional)

1 Make the choux pastry. Put
   75 g (3 oz) of the butter and
200 ml (7 fl oz) water in a saucepan
and bring to the boil.

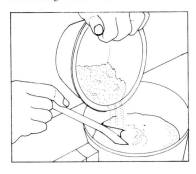

2 Add 100 g (4 oz) of the flour
   all at once, then beat well until
mixture leaves the sides of the
pan. Remove from the heat. Cool
slightly for 5 minutes, then
gradually beat in the eggs.

3 Using a 1 cm (½ inch) plain
   nozzle, pipe the mixture in 2
circles (one on top of the other)
round the bottom of four 200 ml
(7 fl oz) ovenproof dishes. Bake in
the oven at 220°C (425°F) mark 7
for about 25 minutes until risen
and golden brown.

4 Meanwhile, poach the smoked
   haddock in enough water to
cover for 10 minutes. Drain, flake
the flesh and discard the skin and
bones.

5 Melt the remaining butter in a
   saucepan, add the onion and
fry gently for 5 minutes. Add the
remaining flour and cook gently,
stirring, for 1–2 minutes. Remove
from the heat and gradually blend
in the milk. Bring to the boil,
stirring constantly, then simmer
for 3 minutes until thick and
smooth.

6 Stir in the capers, eggs, fish
   and strips of tomato. Add salt,
pepper and lemon juice to taste.

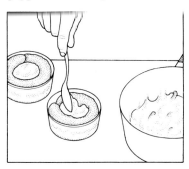

7 Spoon the mixture into the
   centre of the cooked gougères.
Mix together the breadcrumbs
and cheese, sprinkle on top and
return to the oven for a further 10
minutes. Sprinkle with chopped
parsley before serving, if liked.

Menu Suggestion
For a light lunch or supper,
Smoked Haddock Gougères need
no accompaniment other than a
crisp green salad. Chilled dry
cider, white wine or lager would
make the ideal drink.

SMOKED HADDOCK GOUGÈRES

Gougère is a Burgundian
savoury choux pastry dish.
   It may seem unusual to use
choux pastry for a savoury dish,
but the method is just the same
as for sweet choux. When
making this type of pastry, there
are a few points worth
remembering. Measure the
ingredients as accurately as
possible. When beating the flour
into the butter and water at the
beginning of the method, only
beat as long as it takes to make a
smooth mixture. If you overbeat
at this stage, the pastry will not
rise properly during baking.
   Beat the eggs in gradually and
thoroughly. At this stage the
dough can be beaten quite
vigorously, although you should
watch the consistency quite
carefully. Beating should take
approximately 3 minutes; if you
feel that the eggs used are on the
large size and may make the
pastry too sloppy, then do not
add the last of the egg. The
finished dough should be firm,
glossy, and hold its shape.

TURMERIC AND WALNUT MUSHROOMS

0.15*	£ £	514 cals

* plus 8 hours chilling

Serves 8

1.1 kg (2½ lb) button mushrooms

300 ml (½ pint) olive or vegetable oil

100 ml (4 fl oz) white wine vinegar

5 ml (1 tsp) Dijon mustard

5 ml (1 tsp) caster sugar

15 ml (1 tbsp) ground turmeric

1 garlic clove, skinned and crushed

salt and freshly ground pepper

125 g (4 oz) walnut pieces

350 g (12 oz) Emmental, cubed

chopped fresh parsley, to garnish

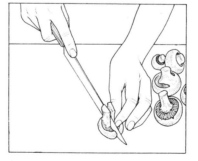

1 Wipe the button mushrooms. Leave the small ones whole and cut any larger ones in half. Put in a serving dish.

2 In a jug, whisk together the oil, vinegar, mustard, sugar, turmeric and crushed garlic until well blended into a dressing. Add salt and pepper to taste.

3 Pour the turmeric dressing over the mushrooms and mix thoroughly to coat. Cover and leave to marinate in the refrigerator for at least 8 hours.

4 To serve, stir the mushrooms well and mix in the walnut pieces and Emmental. Garnish with chopped parsley.

Menu Suggestion

Serve these marinated mushrooms for a light evening meal with fresh wholemeal or granary bread and butter, and a mixed salad. Without the Emmental, they would make an unusual first course for a dinner party.

VEGETARIAN SALAD

| 0.30* | £ | 380 cals |

* plus 30 minutes chilling

Serves 6

225 g (8 oz) hard white (Dutch) cabbage

175 g (6 oz) shelled Brazil nuts

225 g (8 oz) Edam or Gouda, grated

2 large carrots, peeled and grated

60 ml (4 tbsp) natural yogurt

60 ml (4 tbsp) soured cream or mayonnaise

juice of 1 lemon

30 ml (2 tbsp) vegetable oil

30 ml (2 tbsp) chopped fresh parsley

2.5–5 ml ($\frac{1}{2}$–1 tsp) caraway seeds, according to taste

salt and freshly ground pepper

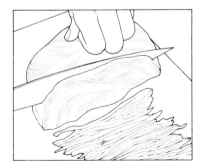

1 Shred the cabbage finely with a sharp knife or grater. Place in a bowl. Chop the nuts roughly. Add the nuts, reserving 30 ml (2 tbsp) for the garnish. Add two-thirds of the cheese to the bowl with the cabbage and carrots.

2 In a separate bowl, mix the yogurt with the soured cream, lemon juice, oil, parsley and caraway seeds. Add salt and pepper to taste.

3 Pour the dressing over the salad ingredients, then toss well to mix. Garnish the top with the reserved nuts and the remaining cheese. Cover the bowl with cling film and chill in the refrigerator for 30 minutes. Taste and adjust seasoning before serving.

Menu Suggestion
Crisp, crunchy Vegetarian Salad makes a delicious lunch dish. Serve with granary rolls.

*J*ANSSON'S *T*EMPTATION

| 2.20 | £ | 317 cals |

Serves 6

1 medium-sized potatoes

two 50 g (2 oz) cans anchovy fillets,
   soaked in milk for 20 minutes
   and drained

1 large onion, skinned

25 g (1 oz) butter or margarine

salt and freshly ground pepper

450 ml (¾ pint) single cream

30 ml (2 tbsp) chopped fresh
   parsley, to garnish

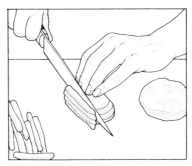

1 Peel the potatoes and cut into
very thin matchstick strips.
Cut the herrings into thin strips.
Chop the onion finely.

2 Arrange half of the potato
strips in a layer in the bottom
of a well-buttered ovenproof dish.
Sprinkle with a little salt and
plenty of pepper.

3 Arrange the strips of anchovy
and chopped onion over the
potato layer, then top with the
remaining potato. Sprinkle with
salt and pepper as before.

4 Pour half the cream slowly
into the dish, then dot with the
remaining butter. Bake in the oven
at 180°C (350°F) mark 4 for 30
minutes. Add the remaining cream
and bake for a further 1 hour or
until the potatoes feel tender when
pierced with a skewer. Cover the
dish with foil if the potatoes show
signs of over-browning during
cooking. Serve hot, sprinkled with
the parsley.

Menu Suggestion

In Sweden, Jansson's
Temptation is served as a starter,
but it is substantial enough to be
served as a meal on its own. To
refresh the palate, follow with a
crisp green salad tossed in a sharp
oil and vinegar dressing.

JANSSON'S TEMPTATION

This tasty dish of fish and
potatoes comes from Sweden,
where it is called *janssons
frestelse*. The name is believed
to have come from a 19th
century Swedish prophet, Erik
Jansson. The story goes that
Jansson was a strict vegetarian
because of his faith, but that this
was one dish he simply couldn't
resist eating.

CELERIAC AU GRATIN

1.00	£ £	351–527 cals

Serves 4–6

15 ml (1 tbsp) lemon juice

2 heads of celeriac, total weight about 900 g (2 lb)

salt and freshly ground pepper

100 g (4 oz) butter or margarine

150 ml ($\frac{1}{4}$ pint) dry white wine

175 g (6 oz) Gruyère, grated

75 g (3 oz) Parmesan, freshly grated

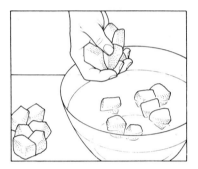

1 Fill a bowl with cold water and add the lemon juice. Peel the celeriac, then cut into chunky pieces. Place the pieces in the bowl of acidulated water as you prepare them, to prevent discoloration.

2 Drain the celeriac, then plunge quickly into a large pan of boiling salted water. Return to the boil and blanch for 10 minutes. Drain thoroughly.

3 Melt the butter in a flame-proof gratin dish. Add the celeriac and turn to coat in the butter. Stir in the wine. Mix together the Gruyère and Parmesan cheeses and sprinkle over the top of the celeriac, with salt and pepper to taste. Bake in the oven at 190°C (375°F) mark 5 for 30 minutes until the celeriac is tender when pierced with a skewer and the topping is golden brown.

Menu Suggestion

Serve for a vegetarian supper dish, with a colourful tomato or red pepper salad, and hot garlic or herb bread.

CELERIAC AU GRATIN

Make the most of celeriac in the winter months; it is a seasonal vegetable which is rarely seen in the shops at other times of year. From the same family as celery, which it resembles in flavour, it is an unusual, quite ugly-looking vegetable, sometimes called "turnip-rooted celery", which is an apt description. Only buy small celeriac, very large specimens tend to be woody and lacking in flavour—and difficult to deal with. This recipe for Celeriac au Gratin has a definite "European" flavour. The French, Swiss and Italians have always used celeriac a lot in their cooking, and on the continent you will come across many different ways of serving it. Steamed or boiled celeriac is usually served as a vegetable accompaniment, simply tossed in melted butter and chopped fresh herbs, or coated in a béchamel or Hollandaise sauce; lightly blanched fingers of celeriac are coated in a vinaigrette dressing while still warm and served as a first course; and grated raw celeriac is served with mayonnaise to make *céléri-rave rémoulade*, a popular French hors d'oeuvre.

The recipe on this page makes a tasty light supper dish, and would make an excellent main course if you are entertaining vegetarians. If you would like to make it more substantial by adding meat, mix 175–225 g (6–8 oz) chopped cooked bacon or ham with the celeriac, before topping with the cheeses.

Carrot and Orange Soup

1.00 £ ✳ 206 cals

Serves 4

700 g (1½ lb) carrots, peeled
1 medium onion, skinned
175 g (6 oz) potatoes, peeled
50 g (2 oz) butter or margarine
2 large oranges
1.1 litres (2 pints) chicken stock
salt and freshly ground pepper
snipped chives, to garnish

1 Slice all the vegetables thinly. Melt the butter in a large, heavy-based saucepan, add the vegetables and fry quickly until just turning colour.

2 Grate in the rind of 1 of the oranges. Add the stock, stir well and bring to the boil.

3 Lower the heat, add salt and pepper to taste, then cover the pan tightly and simmer for 40 minutes until vegetables are soft.

4 Purée the soup in a blender or food processor, then return to the rinsed-out pan. Reheat gently.

5 Squeeze the oranges. Add this juice to the soup and heat well. Taste and season. Sprinkle with chives just before serving.

Menu Suggestion
Serve for a quick supper, with melted cheese on toast.

OEUFS GRUYÈRE

| 0.45 | £ £ | 653 cals |

Serves 4

40 g (1½ oz) butter or margarine

100 g (4 oz) button mushrooms, thinly sliced

40 g (1½ oz) plain flour

150 ml (¼ pint) milk

150 ml (¼ pint) dry white wine

150 ml (¼ pint) double cream

175 g (6 oz) Gruyère, grated

1.25 ml (¼ tsp) ground mace

salt and freshly ground pepper

4 eggs, size 1 or 2

30 ml (2 tbsp) grated Parmesan

2.5 ml (½ tsp) paprika

about 60 ml (4 tbsp) dried breadcrumbs

1 Melt the butter in a saucepan, add the mushrooms and fry gently for 5 minutes. Remove with a slotted spoon and set aside.

2 Add the flour and cook gently, stirring, for 1–2 minutes. Remove from the heat and gradually blend in the milk and wine. Bring to the boil, stirring constantly, then simmer for 3 minutes until thick and smooth.

3 Lower the heat, stir in the cream, 100 g (4 oz) of the Gruyère and cook gently until the cheese melts. Add the mace, salt and pepper and remove from the heat. Stir in the mushrooms.

4 Pour half the sauce into 4 individual gratin dishes. Break an egg in the centre of each dish. Cover with the remaining sauce.

5 Mix the remaining Gruyère with the Parmesan and paprika and sprinkle over the sauce. Cover with breadcrumbs. Bake in the oven at 190°C (375°F) mark 5 for 10–15 minutes. Serve hot.

Menu Suggestion

Oeufs Gruyère are deliciously creamy. Serve for a quick lunch or supper, with a tossed mixed salad.

Christmas Around the World

It's fun to find out what other countries cook at Christmastime, and it helps ring the changes if you can make something a little bit different from the usual traditional fare.

Even though we enjoy our own Christmas specialities, cooking the same things year in year out can eventually lose its appeal. In this chapter, there's a selection of the world's best Christmas dishes; they'll help put the sparkle back in your Christmas cooking.

OLD-FASHIONED PLUM PUDDING
(GREAT BRITAIN)

4.30–5.00* £ ✳ 514 cals

* plus 24 hours standing, 1–2 hours cooling. At least 1 month maturing and 2–3 hours resteaming

Serves 8

100 g (4 oz) prunes, stoned and chopped

175 g (6 oz) currants

175 g (6 oz) seedless raisins

175 g (6 oz) sultanas

25 g (1 oz) blanched almonds, chopped

finely grated rind and juice of 1 lemon

100 g (4 oz) plain flour

2.5 ml ($\frac{1}{2}$ tsp) grated nutmeg

2.5 ml ($\frac{1}{2}$ tsp) ground cinnamon

2.5 ml ($\frac{1}{2}$ tsp) salt

75 g (3 oz) fresh breadcrumbs

100 g (4 oz) shredded suet

100 g (4 oz) dark soft brown sugar

2 eggs, beaten

150 ml ($\frac{1}{4}$ pint) brown ale

150 ml ($\frac{1}{4}$ pint) brandy, rum or sherry

holly sprig, to decorate

brandy or rum butter (page 157) or cream, to serve

75 ml (5 tbsp) brandy, to flame

1 Place the dried fruits in a large bowl with the nuts, lemon rind and juice. Mix well.

2 In a separate bowl, sift together the flour, nutmeg, cinnamon and salt. Add the bread-crumbs, suet and sugar and mix.

3 Pour in the beaten egg and brown ale, beat well, then stir in the dried fruit mixture until evenly incorporated. Cover the bowl with cling film and leave to stand in a cool place for 24 hours.

4 The next day, add the brandy, rum or sherry, stirring well. Butter a 1.7 litre (3 pint) pudding basin and pack in the pudding mixture, pushing it down well.

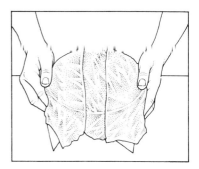

5 Cover the basin with pleated greaseproof paper and foil and secure tightly with string. Place over a large saucepan filled with enough boiling water to come halfway up the sides of the basin. Bring to the boil and steam the pudding for 4–5 hours, topping up with boiling water when necessary.

6 Remove the pudding from the pan and allow to cool com-pletely for 1–2 hours.

7 Uncover the pudding, then re-cover in fresh greaseproof paper and foil. Store in a cool, dry place for at least 1 month (or up to 1 year) before serving.

8 To serve, steam in the same way for 2–3 hours. Turn out on to a warmed serving dish, decorate with a sprig of holly and serve with brandy or rum butter or cream.

9 To flame the pudding, warm the brandy gently in a small saucepan, pour over the pudding and light carefully with a match.

Menu Suggestion
Custard or cream can be served with plum pudding, but brandy or rum butter is more traditional.

TRADITIONAL ROAST TURKEY
(GREAT BRITAIN)

| 5.30–6.30 | £ | 668–834 cals |

Serves 8–10

50 g (2 oz) butter

3 medium onions, skinned and finely chopped

225 g (8 oz) lean veal, minced

175 g (6 oz) lean bacon, rinded and minced

175 g (6 oz) fresh white breadcrumbs

2 large mushrooms, chopped

15 ml (1 tbsp) chopped fresh parsley or 5 ml (1 tsp) dried

2.5 ml ($\frac{1}{2}$ tsp) mace

1.25 ml ($\frac{1}{4}$ tsp) cayenne

salt and freshly ground pepper

1 egg, beaten

100 g (4 oz) suet or 60 ml (4 tbsp) beef dripping

225 g (8 oz) medium oatmeal

4.5–5.5 kg (10–12 lb) turkey

melted dripping or butter, for brushing

1 Make the veal forcemeat stuffing. Melt the butter in a small frying pan, add 1 of the onions and fry gently for 5 minutes.

2 Meanwhile, put the veal and bacon in a bowl and beat well.

3 Stir in the fried onions, breadcrumbs, mushrooms, parsley, mace, cayenne and salt and pepper to taste. Bind with the beaten egg; if the mixture is too stiff, add a little milk. Cool for 20 minutes.

4 Make the oatmeal stuffing. Melt the suet or dripping in a frying pan, add the remaining onions and fry gently for 5 minutes until soft but not coloured. Stir in the oatmeal and cook over a gentle heat, stirring, until the mixture is thick and thoroughly cooked. Add plenty of salt and pepper to taste. Turn into a greased 600 ml (1 pint) pudding basin. Cover with greaseproof paper and foil.

5 Remove the giblets and wash the bird. Drain well and pat dry with absorbent kitchen paper.

6 Stuff the neck end of the turkey with the veal stuffing, taking care not to pack it too tightly. Cover the stuffing smoothly with the neck skin.

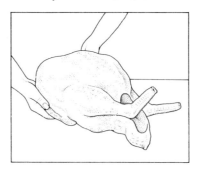

7 With the bird breast side up, fold the wing tips neatly under the body, catching in the neck skin.

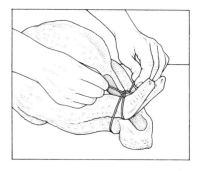

8 Truss the bird and tie the legs together. Make the body as plump and even in shape as possible.

9 Weigh the bird and calculate the cooking time, allowing 20 minutes per 450 g (1 lb) plus 20 minutes. Put the bird breast side up on a rack in a roasting tin. Brush with melted dripping and sprinkle with plenty of salt and pepper.

10 Cover the bird loosely with foil. Roast in the oven at 180°C (350°F) mark 4 for the calculated cooking time until tender, removing the foil and basting the turkey 30 minutes before the end of cooking time. Turn off the oven and leave the turkey to rest for up to 30 minutes before carving. One hour before the end of cooking the turkey; put the oatmeal stuffing to steam.

TRADITIONAL ROAST TURKEY

Turkey has been the traditional meat for Christmas in Britain since the 16th century. Turkeys were in fact brought to England from the New World by a Yorkshireman, William Strickland, and in his home town of Boynton-on-the-Wold, near Bridlington, there is a wooden turkey lectern in his honour in the local church.

In early days, the turkeys were walked to market at Christmastime, sometimes hundreds of miles. To protect their feet during the long journey, they wore leather 'boots', or their feet were painted with tar!

MINCE PIES
(GREAT BRITAIN)

| 0.55 | £ | ✳ | 360 cals |

Makes 8

225 g (8 oz) plain flour

125 g (4 oz) butter or block
  margarine

450 g (1 lb) mixed fruit mincemeat
  (page 150)

1 egg white, lightly beaten

caster sugar

single cream or brandy butter
  (page 157), to serve

1 Sift the flour into a bowl, then
  rub in the butter until the
mixture resembles fine
breadcrumbs. Bind to a firm
dough with about 60 ml (4 tbsp)
water. Knead lightly until just
smooth. Wrap and chill in the
refrigerator for 20 minutes.

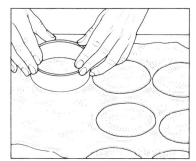

2 Roll out the pastry thinly on a
  floured surface and cut out
sixteen 10 cm (4 inch) rounds, re-
rolling as necessary.

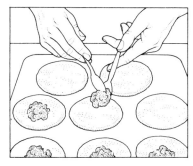

3 Place half of the rounds on
  baking sheets and spoon
mincemeat on to the centre of each.

4 Brush the pastry edges with
  water. Cover with the remaining pastry rounds, sealing the
edges well. Knock up the pastry
edges and flute them if wished.
Bake in the oven at 200°C (400°F)
mark 6 for 15 minutes.

5 Remove the pies from the
  oven, brush with lightly beaten
egg white and dredge with caster
sugar. Repeat the egg and sugar
glaze. Return to the oven for a
further 5–7 minutes.

6 Serve the mince pies hot or
  warm, with single cream or
brandy butter handed separately.

Menu Suggestion
Mince Pies are eaten in Great
Britain throughout the Christmas
period. They can be served as a
dessert, or offered to Christmas
visitors with drinks at any time of
the day.

MINCE PIES
A pretty idea to make mince
pies look more attractive for the
Christmas season, is to decorate
the top of the pies with festive
shapes. Roll out the pastry
trimmings and cut out holly
leaves, then roll little balls of
pastry to make berries. Stick the
shapes on the top of the pies
with water, then paint the leaves
green with edible food colouring,
the berries red.

Roast Duck with Apple Stuffing
(GREAT BRITAIN)

2.30–3.00*	£ £	610 cals

* plus 15 minutes cooling

Serves 4

15 g (½ oz) butter

1 celery stick, trimmed and finely chopped

2 small onions, skinned and chopped

100 g (4 oz) fresh white breadcrumbs

1 small eating apple, peeled, cored and grated

15 ml (1 tbsp) chopped fresh sage or 5 ml (1 tsp) dried

salt and freshly ground pepper

1 egg, beaten

2 kg (4 lb) oven-ready duck (with giblets)

1 bay leaf

15 ml (1 tbsp) plain flour

watercress, to garnish

1 Melt the butter in a saucepan, add the celery and half of the chopped onions and fry gently until soft but not brown.

2 Put the breadcrumbs, apple and sage into a bowl and add the softened celery and onion. Mix very well together, add salt and pepper to taste, then bind with the beaten egg. Cool for 15 minutes.

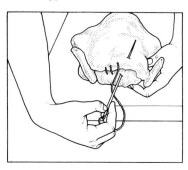

3 Stuff the neck cavity of the duck with this mixture, then sew or truss it together to keep in the stuffing. (If there is too much stuffing for the duck, make the rest into small balls.)

4 Weigh the stuffed duck and calculate the cooking time, allowing 30–35 minutes per 450 g (1 lb). Put the duck on a wire rack in a roasting tin—duck is very fatty and this stops it cooking in its own fat.

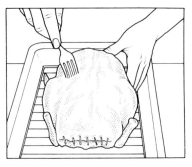

5 Prick the skin of the duck all over to let the fat escape and sprinkle the breast with salt and pepper. Roast in the oven at 180°C (350°F) mark 4 for the calculated cooking time. Cook the stuffing balls in a separate tin on the oven shelf below the duck for the last 30 minutes.

6 While the bird is cooking, make the gravy. Put the giblets in a saucepan with the remaining chopped onion, 600 ml (1 pint) water, the bay leaf and salt and pepper. Simmer for 1 hour; strain.

7 When the duck is cooked, remove from the tin and keep warm in a low oven. Pour off any excess fat from the tin, leaving behind the sediment and about 30 ml (2 tbsp) fat. Transfer to the top of the cooker and blend in the flour. Cook until browned, stirring continuously and scraping any sediment from the bottom of the tin. Slowly stir in the giblet stock and bring to the boil, stirring. Taste and adjust seasoning.

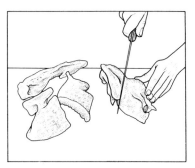

8 To serve, joint the duck into 4 portions, arrange on a warmed serving dish, with the stuffing balls if there are any. Pour the gravy round and garnish with sprigs of watercress. Serve immediately.

Menu Suggestion

Serve roast duck for the Christmas Day meal as an alternative to turkey. It is the traditional bird to serve for a small gathering. The usual trimmings for turkey can be served with duck—roast potatoes, bacon rolls and chipolatas, and Brussels sprouts with chestnuts.

ROAST DUCK WITH APPLE STUFFING

It was the Chinese who first discovered how delicious ducks were to eat, and who first bred the white, or Peking, duck for the table. Now ducks are farmed all over the world, and the duck breeding industry is enormous. Of all the duck breeds, it is the English Aylesbury duck which is the most famous. The Aylesbury duck is believed to be a strain of the original Peking duck, taking its name from the Vale of Aylesbury in Buckinghamshire, where it was originally bred. If you see Aylesbury duckling for sale, then you can be sure of buying a good-quality, meaty bird; the flesh will be tender, and the flavour superb.

OIE RÔTIE AUX PRUNEAUX
(FRENCH ROAST GOOSE WITH PRUNE STUFFING)

| 2.30–3.00* | 🔲 £ £ |

| 480–600 cals |

* plus 10 minutes cooling

Serves 8–10

4–5 kg (9–11 lb) oven-ready
   goose (with giblets)

salt and freshly ground pepper

450 g (1 lb) prunes, soaked
   overnight

300 ml ($\frac{1}{2}$ pint) dry white wine

50 g (2 oz) butter

1 small onion, skinned and finely
   chopped

30 ml (2 tbsp) port

100 g (4 oz) fresh breadcrumbs

5 ml (1 tsp) plain flour

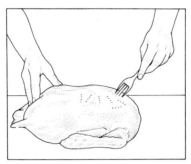

1 Pull inside fat out of the
goose and reserve. Prick the
skin of the goose with a fork in
several places. Rub salt over the
skin.

2 Drain the prunes and place in
a saucepan with the wine.
Bring to the boil and simmer for
about 10 minutes or until tender.
Remove the prunes from the cooking liquid, discard the stones,
chop the flesh and put in a bowl.
Reserve the cooking liquid.

3 Melt 40 g (1$\frac{1}{2}$ oz) of the butter
in another pan, add the onion
and cook gently until soft but not
coloured. Separate the goose liver
from the giblets and chop finely.
Add to the onion and cook gently
for 2–3 minutes, then mix with
the prunes.

4 Deglaze the pan with the port,
scraping the pan to dislodge
any sediment. Pour the liquid into
the prune mixture, add the breadcrumbs and mix well. Allow to
cool for 10 minutes.

5 Spoon the stuffing into the
neck cavity of the goose.
Skewer the neck skin to the back
of the bird, then truss and tie up
the goose with string. Weigh the
bird and calculate the cooking
time, allowing 15 minutes per
450 g (1 lb) plus 15 minutes.

6 Put the goose on a wire rack in
a roasting tin. Cover the breast
with the reserved fat and foil.
Roast in the oven at 200°C
(400°F) mark 6, basting
frequently. Remove the foil for the
last 30 minutes to brown.

7 When the goose is cooked,
transfer to a serving dish and
keep warm in a low oven. Pour off
all but 30 ml (2 tbsp) fat from the
juices in the roasting tin. Transfer
to the top of the cooker and blend
in the flour. Cook for 1 minute
until just colouring, then slowly
add the reserved prune liquid,
stirring well. Bring to the boil and
simmer for 2–3 minutes. Season
to taste and whisk in the remaining butter to give the sauce a good
shine. Serve the sauce separately.

Menu Suggestion
In France, Roast Goose with
Prune Stuffing is a traditional
Christmas meal. Braised onions
and chestnuts are the usual
accompaniments, and you can also
serve roast potatoes and a green
vegetable if liked.

DINDONNEAU AUX MARRONS
(FRENCH ROAST TURKEY WITH CHESTNUT STUFFING)

4.30 | **578–722 cals**

Serves 8–10

700 g (1½ lb) chestnuts

450 ml (¾ pint) chicken stock or water

1 large onion, skinned and roughly chopped

2 celery sticks, trimmed and finely chopped

450 g (1 lb) Toulouse sausage or other spicy pork sausage, skinned and finely chopped

50 ml (2 fl oz) brandy

30 ml (2 tbsp) chopped mixed fresh herbs, e.g. thyme, sage and parsley

salt and freshly ground pepper

1 egg, beaten

4 kg (9 lb) oven-ready turkey

50 g (2 oz) butter

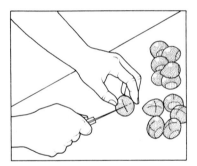

1 Nick the skin of each chestnut with the point of a sharp knife, then plunge the chestnuts into a pan of boiling water. Boil for 15 minutes, then drain.

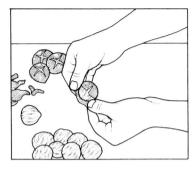

2 Peel the chestnuts, then place in a saucepan with the stock or water, onion and celery. Bring to the boil, then simmer for about 20 minutes until just tender.

3 Remove the chestnuts from the cooking liquid with a slotted spoon. Reserve half of them and work the remainder to a purée in a blender or food processor, with a little of the cooking liquid.

4 Put the puréed chestnuts in a bowl with the chopped sausage, brandy, herbs and salt and pepper to taste. Strain the remaining cooking liquid from the chestnuts and add the onion and celery to the stuffing mixture. Reserve the cooking liquid. Bind the stuffing with the beaten egg.

5 Fill the neck of the turkey with the stuffing, then truss with thread or fine string. Put the turkey on a rack in a roasting tin.

6 Brush all over the bird with the butter and sprinkle liberally with salt and pepper. Pour enough of the reserved chestnut cooking liquid into the tin to just cover the base.

7 Roast the turkey in the oven at 190°C (375°F) mark 5 for 3 hours. Add more chestnut liquid to the tin if it becomes dry during roasting, and add the whole chestnuts and the remaining liquid 30 minutes before the end of the cooking time. If the turkey breast and thighs show signs of over-browning during the roasting time, cover them with foil.

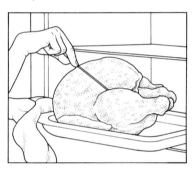

8 To test if the turkey is cooked, pierce the thickest part of a thigh with a skewer—the juices should run clear. When cooked, transfer to a warmed carving dish and leave to stand for 15–30 minutes in a warm place before carving. (Leaving the turkey to stand makes it easier to carve.) Serve the chestnuts around the turkey in the dish and the cooking liquid separately in a gravy boat.

Menu Suggestion

Roast Turkey with Chestnut Stuffing is usually served on Christmas Eve in France. Oysters and champagne are the traditional starter, then the turkey follows with all the trimmings—roast potatoes, Brussels sprouts with chestnuts, giblet gravy and cranberry sauce. The meal comes to a spectacular finale with Bûche de Noël (page 108).

ROAST RIB OF BEEF WITH BATTER PUDDING
(IRELAND)

2.00	🍴	£ £	745 cals

Serves 8

2.7 kg (6 lb) rib of beef

10 ml (2 tsp) dried mixed herbs

freshly ground pepper

225 g (8 oz) plain flour plus 15 ml (1 tbsp)

salt

2 eggs

600 ml (1 pint) milk or milk and water mixed

50 g (2 oz) lard or dripping or 45 ml (3 tbsp) vegetable oil

450 ml (¾ pint) beef stock

1 Weigh the meat and calculate the cooking time. Allow 15 minutes per 450 g (1 lb) plus 15 minutes for rare beef, or 20 minutes per 450 g (1 lb) plus 20 minutes for medium. Place on a wire rack in a roasting tin and sprinkle with the herbs and pepper to taste.

2 Roast the beef in the oven at 180°C (350°F) mark 4 for the calculated cooking time.

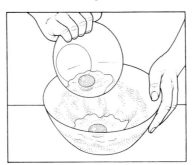

3 To make the batter, mix the 225 g (8 oz) flour and a pinch the centre and add the eggs.

4 Add half of the milk, then gradually mix in the flour with a wooden spoon. Beat the mixture until smooth, then add the remaining milk gradually and beat well. Set aside.

5 Fifty minutes before the beef is ready, heat the dripping or oil in a roasting tin until smoking hot. Pour in the batter and put in the oven, on a shelf above the beef, to cook for 40–45 minutes until well-risen and golden brown. Do not open the oven door for at least 30 minutes or the pudding will sink.

6 When the meat is cooked, transfer to a serving dish and keep warm in a low oven.

7 Pour off all but 30 ml (2 tbsp) fat from the roasting tin. Transfer to the top of the cooker and blend in the 15 ml (1 tbsp) flour. Cook gently to a golden brown, stirring frequently. Gradually blend in the stock, bring to the boil and cook for 3–4 minutes. Season to taste, then strain into a gravy boat.

Menu Suggestion

For those who do not like poultry, this Irish roast beef makes a welcome alternative at Christmas. Serve with all the usual trimmings and the meal will look just as festive.

TOURTIÈRE
(CANADIAN PORK AND VEAL PIE)

1.45	610 cals

Serves 6

50 g (2 oz) butter

2 large onions, skinned and finely chopped

450 g (1 lb) lean boneless pork (eg leg or loin)

450 g (1 lb) boneless veal (eg pie or stewing veal)

150 ml ($\frac{1}{4}$ pint) dry white wine or chicken stock

5 ml (1 tsp) ground allspice

salt and freshly ground pepper

about 25 g (1 oz) fresh breadcrumbs

60–90 ml (4–6 tbsp) chopped fresh parsley and thyme, mixed

150 g (5 oz) shortcrust pastry (page 158)

225 g (8 oz) frozen puff pastry, defrosted

beaten egg, to glaze

1 Melt the butter in a large frying pan, add the onions and fry very gently for 10–15 minutes, stirring frequently, until soft and lightly coloured.

2 Meanwhile, cut the pork and veal into fine dice or thin matchstick lengths. Add to the onions and fry for 10 minutes until changing colour.

3 Stir in the wine or stock, then add the allspice and salt and pepper to taste. Cover and cook gently for 30 minutes, stirring occasionally.

4 Remove the meat and onions from the cooking liquid with a slotted spoon and set aside in a bowl. Boil the liquid in the pan to reduce slightly, then pour over the meat. Add enough breadcrumbs to absorb the liquid, then stir in the herbs. Leave to cool.

5 Meanwhile, roll out the short-crust pastry on a floured surface to a circle to fit a 23.5 cm (9 inch) pie plate.

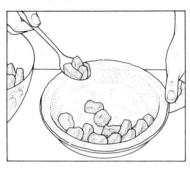

6 Place the pastry circle on the pie plate and pile the cooled meat mixture on top, doming it in the centre.

7 Roll out the puff pastry on a floured surface to a circle slightly larger than the first, to make a lid for the pie.

8 Moisten the rim of shortcrust pastry with water, then place the puff pastry lid on top. Press to seal, then knock up and flute or crimp the edges.

9 Decorate the top of the pie with pastry trimmings and make a hole in the centre for the steam to escape. Brush with beaten egg to glaze.

10 Bake in the oven at 200°C (400°F) mark 6 for 30 minutes until the pastry is golden brown. Serve hot.

Menu Suggestion
Serve Tourtière for supper on Christmas Eve, as the Canadians do. The filling is very meaty and rich, therefore plain accompaniments are best, such as a green vegetable or a green or mixed salad.

TOURTIÈRE
The word *tourtière* originally meant a game pie in French, from the French word *tourte*, meaning a savoury pastry tart. French Canadians often use poultry, pork or veal, and in the French-speaking part of Canada the name *tourtière* is now used to describe the spiced meat pie which is traditionally eaten on Christmas Eve. Pork is usually included in a Christmas *tourtière*.

For a decoration with a difference, spell out the word TOURTIÈRE in letters made from the pastry trimmings. Stick the letters on top of the pie and brush with beaten egg. The letters will retain their shape during baking.

PRUGNE SOTTO SPIRITO
(ITALIAN PLUMS IN GRAPPA)

0.15* £ £ 1582 cals

* plus at least 3 months maturing

Makes about 450 g (1 lb)

about 450 g (1 lb) unblemished ripe plums

4 whole cloves

2.5 cm (1 inch) cinnamon stick

200 g (7 oz) granulated sugar

about 300 ml ($\frac{1}{2}$ pint) grappa (see box)

1 Wash and dry the plums, leaving the stalks on. Put them in a sterilised airtight Kilner or screwtop 1 litre ($1\frac{3}{4}$ pint) glass jar, packing them right to the top. Add the cloves, cinnamon stick and sugar.

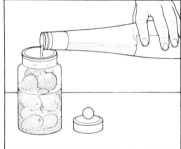

2 Pour in enough grappa to come to the top of the jar and completely cover the fruit. Seal.

3 Leave for at least 3 months before using, shaking the jar gently from time to time during the first month.

PRUGNE SOTTO SPIRITO

Italians serve these plums with espresso coffee whenever visitors drop by. This version uses *grappa*, a kind of rough brandy distilled from the skins, pips and stalks of grapes. Ordinary brandy can be used if *grappa* is difficult to obtain.

FLÆSKESTEG
(DANISH ROAST LOIN OF PORK)

| 2.30 | 813 cals |

Serves 6

1.5 kg (3–3½ lb) boned, rolled and tied loin of pork

salt and freshly ground pepper

2 cooking apples, peeled, cored and cut into eighths

18 'no-need-to-soak' prunes, stoned

15 g (½ oz) plain flour

50 ml (2 fl oz) double cream

1 Score the rind of the pork with a very sharp knife, if the butcher has not already done so. Weigh the joint and calculate the cooking time, allowing 40 minutes per 450 g (1 lb).

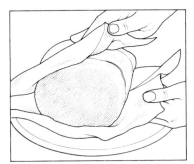

2 Dry the rind thoroughly with absorbent kitchen paper, then rub with 10 ml (2 tsp) salt. Place the joint, rind side uppermost, on a rack in a roasting tin.

3 Roast the pork in a 220°C (425°F) mark 7 oven for 40 minutes, then remove from the oven and pour 300 ml (½ pint) water into the roasting tin, underneath the rack. Return the pork to the oven, lower the temperature to 180°C (350°F) mark 4, and roast for the remaining cooking time, adding the apples and prunes to the water for the last 45 minutes. Do not baste the pork or the crackling will not crisp.

4 Transfer the pork to a carving dish and leave to settle for about 15 minutes before carving. Remove the fruit from the water with a slotted spoon and keep hot.

5 Make a gravy from the pan juices. In a measuring jug, mix the flour to a paste with a little cold water. Stir in more cold water up to the 300 ml (½ pint) mark.

6 Remove the rack from the roasting tin and transfer the tin to the top of the cooker. Stir the flour mixture into the liquid in the tin, a little at a time, then bring to the boil. Simmer, stirring, until thickened, then stir in the cream and salt and pepper to taste. Heat through, then pour into a gravy boat. Serve the pork with the fruit and the gravy handed separately.

Menu Suggestion

For the Christmas meal in Denmark, roast pork is served with *rødkål* (hot red cabbage) and *brunede kartofler* (potatoes which have been boiled then caramelised in butter and sugar).

FLÆKESTEG

The Danes eat roast pork all year round, but this recipe with apples and prunes is traditional for the Christmas meal. There are many regional variations, but the fruit is essential—along with really crisp, crunchy crackling. The Danes serve their Christmas pork hot with vegetables, but you can cook pork by this method for serving cold (without the gravy). A boned, rolled and tied loin of pork makes a neat joint for slicing, which is excellent if you have to cater for a Christmas party.

RISENGRØD
(DANISH CHRISTMAS RICE PUDDING)

| 0.30* | £ | 438–656 cals |

* plus 30–40 minutes cooling and 8 hours chilling

Serves 4–6

568 ml (1 pint) milk

75 g (3 oz) pudding rice

50 g (2 oz) caster sugar

4–5 drops of vanilla flavouring

50 g (2 oz) chopped almonds

1 glass of sherry

300 ml (½ pint) double cream

1 whole almond

chopped almonds, toasted,
  to decorate

Danish Hot Cherry Sauce (see
  right), to serve

1 Put the milk and rice in a saucepan and simmer for about 20 minutes until the rice is soft and most of the milk is absorbed.

2 Add the sugar, vanilla flavouring, almonds and sherry and stir well. Leave to cool completely.

3 Stir in the cream. Transfer to a serving dish and push the whole almond into the pudding so that it is hidden. Cover and chill in the refrigerator for 8 hours. Decorate with the almonds and serve with Danish Hot Cherry Sauce.

KIRSEBAERSAUCE
(DANISH HOT CHERRY SAUCE)

0.20	592 cals

Makes about 600 ml (1 pint)

225 g (8 oz) cherries

110 g (4 oz) granulated sugar

15 ml (1 tbsp) arrowroot

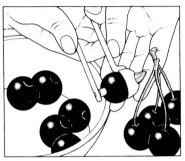

1 Stone the cherries. Put the sugar in a heavy saucepan, add 300 ml ($\frac{1}{2}$ pint) water and heat very gently until the sugar has dissolved.

2 Increase the heat and boil rapidly for 1 minute. Add the cherries and cook them for 10 minutes until tender.

3 Mix the arrowroot with 30 ml (2 tbsp) water and stir into the cherries. Simmer for 2 minutes until the sauce is clear. Serve hot, with Danish Christmas Rice Pudding.

RISENGRØD
This elegant pudding contains sherry, cream and chopped almonds. A single whole almond is always put in the pudding for luck. The finder receives a present and, if single, will be the next to marry.

JULSKINKA
(SWEDISH GLAZED HAM)

4.00*	661–826 cals

* plus overnight soaking, and cooling

~~Serves 8–10~~

9–10 lb (4–4.5 kg) leg of ham (gammon)

10 white peppercorns

10 black peppercorns

few cloves

2 bay leaves

1 egg

15 ml (1 tbsp) granulated sugar

10 ml (2 tsp) mustard powder

60 ml (4 tbsp) dried breadcrumbs, to coat

1 Soak the gammon in cold water overnight. When ready to cook, drain and place fat side uppermost in a very large saucepan. Cover with fresh cold water and add the peppercorns, cloves and bay leaves.

2 Bring slowly to the boil, then skim the scum off the surface with a slotted spoon. Lower the heat, cover and simmer for 3–3½ hours until tender when pierced with a skewer (do not overcook or the ham will be dry).

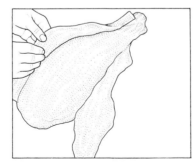

3 Remove the gammon from the liquid and carefully strip off the rind, leaving the fat intact. Pat with absorbent kitchen paper to remove excess fat, then return to the liquid and leave until cold.

4 Remove the gammon from the liquid, drain thoroughly and pat dry. Place in a roasting tin. Put the egg in a bowl with the sugar and mustard powder and beat well to mix.

5 Brush the glaze over the exposed gammon fat, then press breadcrumbs on top until evenly coated. Pour a few tablespoonfuls of the cooking liquid into the tin and grill the ham for a few minutes to toast the topping. Serve cold.

JULSKINKA

In Sweden, Julskinka ham is served as part of the traditional smørgasbörd or cold table on Christmas Eve. Many Swedish cooks go to town on the decoration of the ham, which makes a spectacular table centrepiece, especially when finished off with a large paper frill as in the photograph here. The orange segments and clusters of green and black grapes are traditional, although some people prefer a garnish of prunes, or poached apple halves filled with redcurrant jelly. Cumberland sauce is sometimes served as an accompaniment to Julskinka, but this is a matter of personal taste.

On Christmas Eve, most Swedish housewives are too busy during the day to think about cooking ordinary meals for their family. As a result, the custom of *dopp i gryten* or 'dip in the pot' has evolved. Beef stock and seasonings are added to the liquid in which the Julskinka has cooked, and hungry members of the family help themselves, by dipping hunks of thick rye bread into it.

Christmas Eve Menu

Plan to get present wrapping and preparations for the Christmas day meal out of the way early on Christmas Eve, so that you can relax at home with a few friends. Offer them a Champagne Cocktail when they arrive, then serve this beautifully decorated Salmon and Asparagus Mousse as the evening wears on. It will get the Christmas festivities off to a glamorous start.

SALMON AND ASPARAGUS MOUSSE

| 0.45* | ⊟ ⊟ | £ £ | 265 cals |

* plus 1¾ hours setting time

Serves 8

25 g (1 oz) aspic powder

25 g (1 oz) butter

25 g (1 oz) plain flour

300 ml (½ pint) milk

1.25 ml (¼ tsp) mustard powder

pinch of cayenne

salt and freshly ground pepper

15 ml (1 tbsp) cider vinegar

3 eggs, separated

two 220 g (7½ oz) cans salmon, drained and flaked

22.5 ml (1½ tbsp) gelatine

150 ml (¼ pint) double cream, lightly whipped

225 g (8 oz) packet frozen asparagus, cooked and cooled

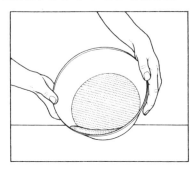

1 Make up the aspic jelly with 600 ml (1 pint) water according to packet instructions. Leave until just on the point of setting, then pour a little into a 20.5 cm (8 inch) spring-release cake tin fitted with a plain base, or into a 1.7-litre (3-pint) fluted mould. Use the jelly to coat the sides of the tin, then chill in the refrigerator for about 20 minutes until set.

2 When set, pour more aspic jelly into the tin until it is 0.5 cm (¼ inch) deep. Chill again for about 20 minutes until set.

7 Pour half of the mixture into a blender or food processor and work until smooth. Turn out and repeat with remainder. Leave for about 30 minutes until just beginning to set.

8 Lightly whip the cream and fold into the mixture. Whisk the egg whites until just holding soft peaks, then fold in carefully until evenly incorporated. Spoon into the tin. Cover and chill in the refrigerator for at least 1 hour until set.

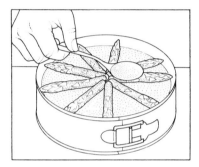

9 When set, arrange the asparagus spears on top. Spoon the remaining aspic jelly over and leave in a cold place for 30 minutes until set.

3 Meanwhile, put the butter in a blender or food processor with the flour, milk, mustard, cayenne and salt and pepper to taste. Work until smooth.

4 Pour into a saucepan, bring to the boil and cook for 3 minutes, stirring constantly. Remove from the heat, beat in the vinegar and then the egg yolks.

5 Return the mixture to the heat and cook gently without boiling for a further 2–3 minutes. Remove from the heat, stir in the drained salmon and check the seasoning.

6 Put 90 ml (6 tbsp) liquid aspic in a small heatproof bowl. Sprinkle in the gelatine and leave to stand for 5 minutes until spongy. Stand the bowl in a saucepan of gently simmering water until the gelatine is dissolved. Add to the salmon mixture.

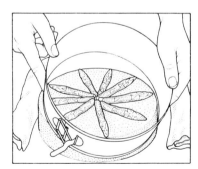

10 To unmould, hold a warm cloth round the sides of the tin, release the clip and remove the ring. Warm the base and slide the mousse on to a serving plate.

Menu Suggestion
Serve with Melba toast and butter curls, and a selection of salads. A potato salad would go well, and a contrasting crunchy celery, apple and walnut salad.

CHAMPAGNE COCKTAIL

| 0.05 | £ £ | 116–154 cals |

Serves 6–8

6–8 small sugar lumps
Angostura bitters
juice of 1½–2 lemons, strained
90–120 ml (6–8 tbsp) brandy
1 bottle of champagne, chilled
wafer-thin lemon slices,
**   to decorate (optional)**

1 Put 1 sugar lump in the bottom of 6–8 tall champagne flutes and pour 4 dashes of Angostura bitters over each.

2 Add the strained lemon juice and brandy to each and top up with champagne. Float a thin slice of lemon on top of each glass, if liked. Serve immediately.

Alternative Christmas

It's not every year that
you want the same
traditional fare at
Christmastime. Maybe
there are less of you than
usual, or maybe you
simply feel like a change.
This menu will fit the bill
whatever the reason, and
can easily be adapted to
serve different numbers,
from as few as two, to
as many as six.

PRAWNS WITH AVOCADO DRESSING

| 0.45* | £ £ | 444–666 cals |

* plus up to 2 hours chilling

Serves 4–6

30 ml (2 tbsp) olive oil

1 small onion, skinned and finely chopped

2 celery sticks, trimmed and finely chopped

5 ml (1 tsp) paprika

2 ripe avocados

75 ml (3 fl oz) thick homemade mayonnaise (page 157)

75 ml (3 fl oz) double or whipping cream

350 g (12 oz) peeled prawns, defrosted and thoroughly dried if frozen

finely grated rind and juice of 1 lime or lemon

few drops of Tabasco sauce, to taste

salt and freshly ground pepper

lettuce leaves, to serve

unpeeled prawns and lime twists, to garnish (optional)

1 Heat the oil in a small saucepan, add the onion and fry gently until soft but not coloured. Add the celery and paprika and fry, stirring, for 1–2 minutes. Transfer to a bowl and cool.

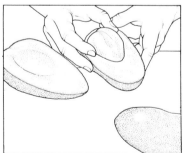

2 Meanwhile, halve, stone and peel 1 of the avocados and mash the flesh in a bowl. Gradually work in the mayonnaise until evenly combined, then stir in the onion and celery mixture.

3 Whip the cream until it holds its shape. Fold the prawns into the avocado mixture, then the cream. Add the lime rind, with Tabasco and salt and pepper to taste. Cover the bowl with cling film and chill in the refrigerator for up to 2 hours before serving. (Do not leave for longer or the avocado may discolour the dressing.)

4 To serve, line one large dish, or 4–6 glasses with shredded lettuce leaves and sprinkle with salt and pepper. Pile the prawn salad in the centre.

5 Halve, stone and peel the remaining avocado and slice neatly. Arrange on top of the salad in a decorative pattern and sprinkle with the lime juice. Serve immediately, garnished with unpeeled prawns and lime twists, if liked.

Menu Suggestion
Serve this rich starter with thinly sliced wholemeal bread and butter. Champagne or a sparkling dry white wine would be the most appropriate drink.

ROAST PHEASANT

| 1.05 | 🍳 | £ £ | 308–461 cals |

Serves 4–6

1 brace of pheasants, plucked and drawn

50 g (2 oz) butter

salt and freshly ground pepper

6 rashers of streaky bacon

25 ml (5 tsp) plain flour

450 ml (¾ pint) chicken stock

gravy browning

15–30 ml (1–2 tbsp) medium dry sherry

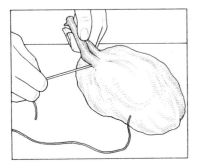

1 Wipe the pheasants and pat dry with absorbent kitchen paper. Place a good knob of butter inside each bird with plenty of salt and pepper. Truss the birds.

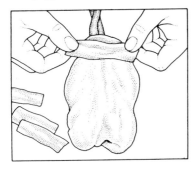

2 Remove the rind from the bacon. Cut each rasher in half, then lay over the breasts of the birds to protect them.

3 Melt the remaining butter in a small roasting tin. Put the birds in the tin and roast in the oven at 200°C (400°F) mark 6 for about 35 minutes depending on size, basting frequently.

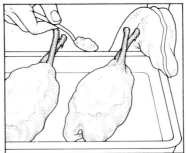

4 Remove the bacon and keep it warm. Brush the breasts with some of the cooking juices and sprinkle 5 ml (1 tsp) flour over each bird. Return to the oven for another 10 minutes.

5 Remove the trussing strings and place the pheasants on a warmed serving dish. Keep warm, uncovered.

6 Pour off all but 30 ml (2 tbsp) fat from the roasting tin and place the tin on top of the cooker. Sprinkle the remaining flour into the residual fat, stir until blended and smooth, then fry gently until russet-coloured, stirring frequently.

7 Stir in the stock gradually, add salt and pepper to taste and bring to the boil. Cook for 3–4 minutes, add a drop of gravy browning if necessary, then stir in the sherry.

8 Garnish the pheasants with the bacon pieces and serve the gravy separately.

Menu Suggestion
The traditional accompaniments are bread sauce (page 156), game chips and Brussels sprouts.

MINCEMEAT TART

| `1.30*` | 🍳 | ✳* | `662–993 cals` |

* plus chilling and cooling; freeze before baking at step 7

Serves 4–6

225 g (8 oz) plain flour

pinch of salt

100 g (4 oz) ground almonds

100 g (4 oz) caster sugar

100 g (4 oz) butter

1 egg, beaten

225 g (8 oz) mincemeat (page 150)

50 g (2 oz) slivered or flaked almonds, chopped

30 ml (2 tbsp) almond-flavoured liqueur, rum or brandy

1 medium cooking apple

45–60 ml (3–4 tbsp) apricot jam, to glaze

single cream or vanilla ice cream, to serve

1 Make the almond pastry. Sift the flour and salt onto a marble slab or other cold surface and stir in the almonds and sugar. Make a well in the centre.

2 Cut the butter into small dice and place in the centre of the flour. Work with the fingertips, gradually drawing the flour mixture into the centre and rubbing it into the butter. Stir in the beaten egg.

3 Gather the dough together and form into a rough ball. (The dough is rich and quite sticky, so work as quickly and lightly as possible, with cold hands.) Wrap the ball of dough in foil and chill in the refrigerator for 30 minutes.

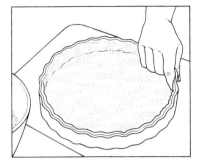

4 Reserve a little dough for the lattice. With your fingertips, press the remaining dough into a 20.5 cm (8 inch) loose-bottomed flan tin standing on a baking sheet. Chill in the refrigerator for a further 15 minutes.

5 Meanwhile, prepare the filling. Put the mincemeat in a bowl with the chopped almonds and liqueur. Peel and core the apple, then grate into the bowl. Stir well to mix, then spoon into the chilled flan case. Level the surface.

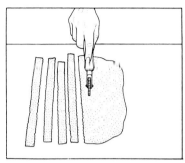

6 Roll out the reserved dough and cut into strips for the lattice, using a pastry wheel to give a pretty edge.

7 Place the strips over the filling in a lattice pattern, then seal the edges with water. Bake in the oven at 190°C (375°F) mark 5 for 35 minutes until the pastry is a light golden brown.

8 Leave the filling to settle for 10–15 minutes. Heat the apricot jam gently in a saucepan, then sieve and brush over the top of the tart to glaze. Leave for a further 10–15 minutes and serve warm or cold, with single cream or scoops of vanilla ice cream.

Menu Suggestion
Mincemeat Tart makes the most delicious dessert with cream or ice cream, but it is just as good served plain as a teatime cake.

MINCEMEAT TART

As its name suggests, mincemeat was originally made with minced meat. The combination of fruit, spices and a large amount of alcohol had a preservative effect on the meat, which was stored in stone crocks, and always left to mature from at least the beginning of December. Beef, tongue and venison were the usual meats included in mincemeat, but nowadays only fruit is used, and shredded beef suet is added to make up for the lack of meat. If you can spare the time, it is much better to make your own mincemeat for Christmas, to be sure of knowing exactly what goes into it. Many commercial brands have far too much suet and a watery flavour and texture, although some of the more expensive varieties do contain plump fruit and a fair amount of alcohol. Read the label carefully before buying, and inspect the contents through the glass jar if possible.

Boxing Day

It's all too easy to forget the food for Boxing Day. Everyone's interest focuses on Christmas Day, so that sometimes the day after can be a sorry affair, with nothing more than leftovers. Plan ahead and freeze Celeriac and Stilton Soup well before the Christmas rush, then you will have plenty of time on Boxing Day morning to turn the leftover turkey into a fresh-looking salad, with the addition of such mouthwatering ingredients as pineapple, soured cream and crisp, crunchy celery.

CELERIAC AND STILTON SOUP

| 1.10 | ❄* | 283 cals |

* freeze at the end of step 5

Serves 8

50 g (2 oz) butter

2 leeks, trimmed, washed and
    roughly chopped

juice of 1 lemon

2 celeriac, total weight about
    900 g (2 lb)

1.7 litres (3 pints) vegetable stock
    (made with cubes)

10 ml (2 tsp) rubbed fresh sage or
    5 ml (1 tsp) dried

salt and freshly ground pepper

225 g (8 oz) Blue Stilton, rinded and
    roughly chopped

300 ml ($\frac{1}{2}$ pint) single cream

fresh sage leaves, to garnish

1 Melt the butter in a large
saucepan, add the leeks and fry
very gently for 10 minutes until
softened.

2 Meanwhile, fill a bowl with
cold water and add the lemon
juice to acidulate it. Peel the
celeriac thickly with a sharp knife.
Cut into chunks, dropping them
into the bowl of acidulated water.

3 Drain the celeriac, then add to
the pan of leeks. Fry gently,
for a further 10 minutes.

4 Add the stock and bring to the
boil, stirring, then add the sage
and salt and pepper to taste.
Lower the heat, cover and simmer
for about 20 minutes or until the
celeriac is very soft.

5 Crumble the Stilton cheese
into a blender or food processor. Add the soup and work to
a smooth purée. (You may have to
work in batches, according to the
size of your machine.)

6 Return the soup to the rinsed-
out pan and stir in the cream.
Reheat, stirring, then taste and
adjust seasoning. Pour into
warmed individual bowls and
garnish with sage leaves. Serve hot.

Menu Suggestion
Serve with warm bread rolls and
butter, or with hot herb bread.

TURKEY, PINEAPPLE AND PASTA SALAD

| 0.30* | 528 cals |

* plus 2 hours chilling

Serves 6

700 g ($1\frac{1}{2}$ lb) cooked turkey meat

45 ml (3 tbsp) olive or vegetable oil

30 ml (2 tbsp) lemon juice

paprika

salt and freshly ground pepper

225 g (8 oz) wholemeal pasta
    shapes

1 small pineapple

300 ml ($\frac{1}{2}$ pint) soured cream

30 ml (2 tbsp) horseradish sauce

10 ml (2 tsp) tomato purée

225 g (8 oz) celery, trimmed and
    finely sliced

25 g (1 oz) salted peanuts

1 Cut the turkey into bite-sized
pieces. In a large bowl, mix
together the oil, lemon juice,
2.5 ml ($\frac{1}{2}$ tsp) paprika and salt and
pepper to taste. Stir in the turkey,
cover and leave in a cool place for
about 1 hour.

2 Meanwhile, cook the pasta as
directed on the packet, drain
and rinse well under cold water.

3 Prepare the pineapple. With a
sharp knife, cut off the leafy
top and discard. Cut the pineapple
into 1 cm ($\frac{1}{2}$ inch) slices. Cut off
the skin and dig out the 'eyes' with
the tip of the knife.

4 Cut out the core from each
slice with an apple corer or
small biscuit cutter. Cut the flesh
into chunks.

5 Put the soured cream in a
large bowl, add the horseradish and tomato purée and stir
well to mix. Fold in the pasta,
celery and pineapple, with salt and
pepper to taste.

6 Stir the turkey into the pasta
mixture, cover and chill in the
refrigerator for at least 1 hour.
Taste and adjust seasoning.
Transfer to a serving dish and
garnish with peanuts and paprika.
Serve chilled.

Menu Suggestion
This meaty salad is quite
substantial. Serve with a leafy
green salad such as lettuce,
chicory and watercress, tossed in a
vinaigrette dressing.

Christmastime Parties

Christmas is the time for large gatherings. A wonderful time for socialising, but sometimes a worrying and exhausting time for the one who's providing the eats. In this chapter there are lots of ideas which should make the catering plain sailing. They're all dishes that can be made well ahead of time, and which can feed large numbers, so that when it comes to party time, you can relax and enjoy yourself too.

GLAZED GAMMON

3.15* | 465 cals

* plus at least 3 hours or overnight
soaking and cooling

Serves 12

2.3 kg (5 lb) joint of gammon
1 onion, skinned
whole cloves
1 carrot, peeled
1 teaspoon ground mixed spice
6 black peppercorns
2 bay leaves
60 ml (4 tbsp) red wine or red wine vinegar
60 ml (4 tbsp) brandy
juice of 1 large lemon
30 ml (2 tbsp) redcurrant jelly
watercress and spiced peaches, to garnish (optional)

1 Soak the gammon joint in several changes of water for at least 3 hours, preferably overnight. Drain, then weigh and calculate the cooking time, allowing 25 minutes per 450 g (1 lb), plus 25 minutes.

2 Put the gammon into a very large saucepan. Add the onion stuck with a few cloves, the carrot, mixed spice, peppercorns, bay leaves and wine or wine vinegar.

3 Pour in enough cold water to cover the gammon and bring to the boil. Lower the heat, cover and simmer for half of the calculated cooking time. Remove from the pan and discard the liquid.

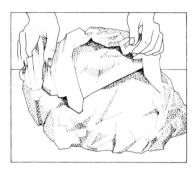

4 With a sharp knife, strip the skin off the gammon while still hot. Wrap the joint in foil and bake in the oven at 180°C (350°F) mark 4 for all but 30 minutes of the remaining cooking time. Unwrap the joint.

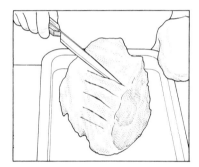

5 With the point of a sharp knife, score a diamond pattern in the fat. Insert cloves into the intersections of the diamonds.

6 Put the brandy, lemon juice and redcurrant jelly in a small heavy-based saucepan and heat gently until the jelly has melted. Boil until reduced to a glaze, then quickly brush over the exposed fat. Return to the oven, increase the temperature to 220°C (425°F) mark 7 and cook for a further 30 minutes. Serve cold, garnished with spiced peaches.

Menu Suggestion
Glazed Gammon makes an impressive table centrepiece for a buffet party. Cut a few slices of gammon, then leave the rest for guests to help themselves.

PARTY PÂTÉ

2.45*	£ £	✳	305–381 cals

* plus cooling and chilling for 1–3 days

Serves 8–10

225 g (8 oz) belly pork, rind and bone removed

225 g (8 oz) chicken livers

100 g (4 oz) fresh white crustless bread

225 g (8 oz) pork sausagemeat

30 ml (2 tbsp) juniper berries, crushed

30 ml (2 tbsp) cranberry sauce

2.5 ml ($\frac{1}{2}$ tsp) grated nutmeg

120 ml (8 tbsp) brandy

2 oranges

salt and freshly ground pepper

1 egg, beaten

450 g (1 lb) boneless game (eg breast of pheasant or rabbit)

orange slices and whole juniper berries, to garnish

1 Mince the belly pork with the chicken livers and bread, or work in a food processor. Turn into a bowl, add the sausagemeat, juniper berries, cranberry sauce, nutmeg and half of the brandy.

2 Mix well together. Grate the rind and squeeze the juice of 1 of the oranges. Add to the pâté mixture with salt and pepper to taste, then bind with beaten egg.

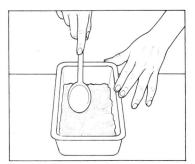

3 Put half of the pâté mixture into a greased and base-lined 1 kg (2 lb) loaf tin, pressing it down with the back of the spoon.

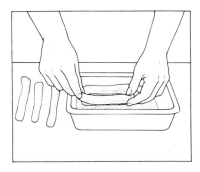

4 Cut the game into thin, even slices and arrange over the pâté mixture. Cover with the remaining pâté and press down.

5 Cover the tin with lightly oiled foil. Stand it in a roasting tin half filled with hot water. Bake at 170°C (325°F) mark 3 for 2 hours.

6 Lift the dish out of the water and place heavy weights on top of the foil covering. Leave until cold, then refrigerate for 1–3 days before serving.

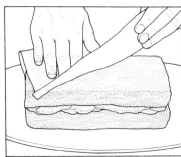

7 To serve, unmould onto a serving plate and wipe away excess fat with absorbent kitchen paper. Squeeze the juice of the remaining orange and pour into a small heavy-based pan. Add the remaining brandy and boil rapidly until reduced. Brush all over the pâté and garnish with orange slices and juniper berries.

Menu Suggestion

Serve this strongly-flavoured pâté with granary French bread and a full-bodied red wine.

TURKEY TERRINE

2.00*	£	✳	311–415 cals

* plus 2 hours cooling and overnight chilling

Serves 6–8

| 225 g (8 oz) cooked turkey meat |
| 225 g (8 oz) turkey or pig's liver |
| 175 g (6 oz) thinly sliced streaky bacon rashers, rinded |
| 1 medium onion |
| 225 g (8 oz) sausagemeat |
| 1 garlic clove, skinned and crushed |
| 15 ml (1 tbsp) chopped fresh sage or 5 ml (1 tsp) dried |
| 45 ml (3 tbsp) double cream |
| 30 ml (2 tbsp) brandy |
| 1 egg |
| salt and freshly ground pepper |
| bay leaf |

1 Mince the turkey, liver, 50 g (2 oz) of the bacon and the onion. (Alternatively, work in a food processor.)

2 Put the minced mixture in a bowl. Add the sausagemeat, garlic, sage, cream, brandy, egg and salt and pepper to taste. Mix with a spoon until all the ingredients are evenly combined.

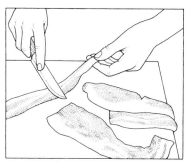

3 Stretch the remaining bacon rashers with the flat side of a blade of a large cook's knife.

4 Use the bacon rashers to line a 1.1 litre (2 pint) terrine or loaf tin, making sure there are no gaps.

5 Spoon the meat mixture into the container and place a bay leaf on top. Cover tightly with foil or a lid, then stand the container in a roasting tin.

6 Pour 3.5 cm ($1\frac{1}{2}$ inches) hot water into the roasting tin, then bake in the oven at 170°C (325°F) mark 3 for about $1\frac{1}{2}$ hours. Remove from the water bath and leave to cool for 2 hours. Place heavy weights on top of the terrine and chill in the refrigerator overnight.

7 To serve, turn the terrine out of the container onto a plate and cut into slices.

Menu Suggestion
Turkey Terrine is a good dish for a buffet party because it is so easy to serve. A selection of salads would be the best accompaniments, especially the Red Cabbage and Beetroot Salad and the Leek and Sprout Salad, on page 154.

TURKEY TERRINE
The method of baking a terrine in a roasting tin with hot water, called a *bain marie* or water bath, is essential if the mixture is to cook properly—the hot water distributes the oven heat evenly through the mixture and gives a moist result. Special water baths can be bought at kitchen equipment shops, but an ordinary roasting tin does the job just as well, and can be used in the oven or on top of the cooker according to individual recipe instructions. Always cover the mixture tightly with foil when cooking in a water bath, or the top of the terrine will form an unpleasant hard crust.

GALANTINE OF DUCKLING

3.00* 🥡 🥡 £ £ ✳ 405 cals

* plus 2 hours cooling and 8 hours chilling

Serves 8

2 kg (4½ lb) oven-ready duckling

225 g (8 oz) minced pork

225 g (8 oz) minced veal

125 g (4 oz) fresh breadcrumbs

125 g (4 oz) sliced cooked ham, roughly chopped

8 stuffed green olives, roughly chopped

finely grated rind of 1 orange

10 ml (2 tsp) chopped fresh sage or 2.5 ml (½ tsp) dried

salt and freshly ground pepper

1 egg, beaten

fresh sage sprigs, to garnish

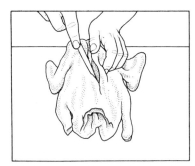

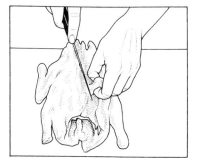

1 Remove the giblets and place the duckling breast side down on a board. Using a small, sharp knife, cut straight along the back bone through the skin and flesh.

2 Start the boning from 1 side of the duckling. Carefully fillet and scrape the flesh and skin away from the rib cage (see above). Ease out the 'oyster' (the small pad of flesh at either side of the back bone. See above right).

3 As the leg joint is reached, locate and loosen the ball and socket joint with the point of the knife. Sever the ligaments to free the leg from the carcass. Loosen the ball and socket wing joint in the same way. Cut out the narrow bone protruding above the wing joint, scraping clear of the flesh.

4 Ease the skin and flesh away from the carcass and detach the leg and wing joints from the other side of the bird.

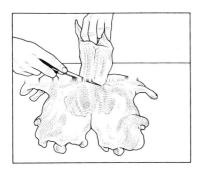

5 Scrape the flesh away from the breast bone, cutting closely against the ridge of the breast bone to free the carcass. Be very careful not to puncture the skin around the breast bone or the stuffing will ooze out.

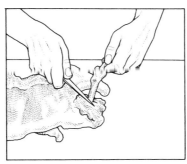

6 With the duckling skin side down, loosen the exposed tips of the leg bones. Gradually scrape and push the flesh off the bones. Work around the hinge joint and then pull the leg completely inside out, detaching the bone from the flesh as far down as possible. Snip away sinews and then push the flesh back into the leg skin.

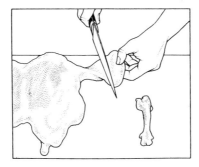

7 Snap the wing joints open. Push and scrape the flesh off the first joint. Ease out this bone and chop off wings at elbows. Trim any excess skin and fat from both ends of the duckling. Retain sufficient skin to sew around the stuffing.

8 Make the stuffing. Put the minced pork and veal in to a large bowl with the breadcrumbs. Add the ham, olives, orange rind, sage and plenty of salt and pepper. Mix well, then bind with the beaten egg.

9 Spoon a little stuffing into the leg cavities, pressing it in firmly. Mound the remaining stuffing in the centre of the body section.

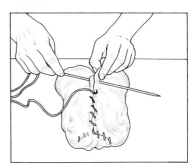

10 Using a needle and fine string or cotton, sew up the body and wing cavities with neat, overlapping stitches. Turn the bird over, breast side up, push back into shape and secure with skewers.

11 Weigh the duckling and calculate the cooking time, allowing 25 minutes per 450 g (1 lb). Place on a rack placed over a roasting tin. Sprinkle with salt. Roast in the oven for the calculated cooking time at 180°C (350°F) mark 4, basting occasionally.

12 When the duckling is cooked, the juices should run clear when the bird is pierced with a fine skewer. Cool for at least 2 hours, then chill in the refrigerator for 8 hours or over-night. To serve, ease out string and slice. Garnish with sprigs of sage.

Menu Suggestion
Galantine of Duckling is a splendid dish for a cold table. Serve with the usual buffet party salads, and with Orange and Apple Chutney (page 156).

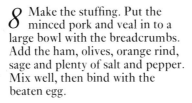

SMOKED SALMON QUICHE

`1.00*` £ £ ✳* `336–420 cals`

* plus 30 minutes chilling; freeze
for 1 month only

Serves 8–10

225 g (8 oz) plain flour

salt and freshly ground pepper

115 g (4 oz) butter or margarine

1 egg yolk

10 ml (2 tsp) lemon juice

about 30 ml (2 tbsp) cold water

175 g (6 oz) full-fat soft cheese

300 ml (½ pint) single or double
  cream

3 eggs

175 g (6 oz) smoked salmon pieces

finely grated rind of 1 lemon

5 ml (1 tsp) paprika

1 Sift the flour and a pinch of salt together into a bowl. Cut the butter into small pieces and add to the flour.

2 Lightly rub in the butter with your fingertips until the mixture resembles fine breadcrumbs.

3 Add the egg yolk and half of the lemon juice, then add enough water to bind the mixture together in large lumps.

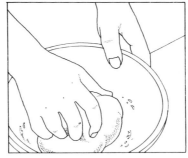

4 With 1 hand, collect the mixture together to form a ball. Knead lightly for a few seconds to give a firm, smooth dough. Do not overhandle.

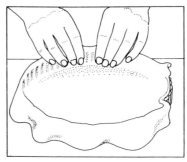

5 Roll out the dough on a floured surface and use to line a 25.5 cm (10 inch) loose-bottomed metal flan tin. Chill in the refrigerator for 30 minutes.

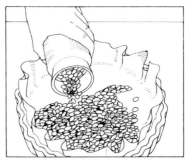

6 Prick the pastry base and then line with foil and fill with baking beans. Bake blind on a preheated baking sheet in the oven at 200°C (400°F) mark 6 for 10 minutes. Remove the foil and beans and return to the oven for a further 5 minutes.

7 Prepare the filling. Put the cheese in a bowl and gradually whisk in the cream. When well mixed and smooth, add the eggs and beat well to mix.

8 Add the salmon, grated lemon rind and remaining lemon juice. Season with a little salt and plenty of pepper, then add half of the paprika and beat well to mix.

9 Pour the filling into the baked flan case and bake in the oven at 190°C (375°F) mark 5 for 25–30 minutes until set. Sprinkle with the remaining paprika while very hot. Serve warm or cold.

Menu Suggestion
Serve for a buffet, with champagne and salads.

WATERCRESS AND RICOTTA QUICHE

| 1.00* | ✳ | 402–536 cals |

* plus 30 minutes chilling

Serves 6–8

pastry made with 225 g (8 oz)
   flour (see left)

50 g (2 oz) butter or margarine

1 bunch of spring onions, trimmed
   and finely chopped

2 bunches of watercress

100 g (4 oz) Ricotta or curd cheese

300 ml (½ pint) single or double
   cream (or whipping)

3 eggs, beaten

2.5 ml (½ tsp) grated nutmeg

salt and freshly ground pepper

1 Line a 25.5 cm (10 inch) loose-
bottomed metal flan tin with
the pastry. Bake blind on a preheated baking sheet (see left).

2 Prepare the filling. Melt the
butter in a saucepan, add the
spring onions and fry gently for
about 5 minutes until softened.
Add the watercress and fry for a
few minutes more, stirring
frequently.

3 Transfer the contents of the
pan to a blender or food processor. Add the next 4 ingredients
with salt and pepper to taste and
work until smooth and evenly
blended.

4 Pour the filling into the baked
flan case and bake in the oven
at 190°C (375°F) mark 5 for 25–30
minutes until set. Serve warm or
leave until cold.

Menu Suggestion
Watercress and Ricotta Quiche
has quite a hot and spicy 'kick'
to it. Serve as part of a buffet
party spread with mayonnaise- or
cream-based salads.

PRAWN AND MUSHROOM BOUCHÉES

1.30* 🗋 £ £ 174 cals

* plus cooling time

Makes 64

100 ml (4 fl oz) dry white wine

75 g (3 oz) butter or margarine

450 g (1 lb) peeled prawns, thawed

225 g (8 oz) button mushrooms,
  wiped and thinly sliced

75 g (3 oz) plain flour

568 ml (1 pint) milk

300 ml (½ pint) double cream

225 g (8 oz) Gruyère or Emmental

60 ml (4 tbsp) grated Parmesan

salt and freshly ground pepper

four 397 g (14 oz) packets frozen
  puff pastry, thawed

beaten egg, to glaze

chopped fresh parsley, unshelled
  prawns and lemon twists,
  to garnish

1 First make the filling. Pour the
wine into a small, heavy-
based saucepan and bring to the
boil. Boil rapidly until reduced to
15 ml (1 tbsp). Remove from heat.

2 Melt the butter in a clean large
saucepan, add the mushrooms
and prawns and fry over moderate
heat, stirring constantly, for about
5 minutes. Remove with a slotted
spoon and drain on absorbent
kitchen paper.

3 Add the flour to the juices in
the pan and cook gently,
stirring, for 1–2 minutes. Remove
from the heat and gradually blend
in the milk. Bring to the boil,
stirring constantly, then simmer
for 3 minutes until thick and
smooth.

4 Add the cream and reduced
white wine, then the Gruyère
and Parmesan. Simmer, stirring,
until the cheese melts, then remove
from the heat and fold in the
drained prawns and mushrooms.
Season with plenty of salt and
pepper, cover with cling film and
leave to go cold.

5 Meanwhile, make the bouchée
cases. Roll out each packet of
pastry to an oblong 24.5 × 23 cm
(9½ × 9 inches).

6 Using a plain 5 cm (2 inch)
round or oval cutter, cut out
16 rounds from each oblong. Place
the rounds on dampened baking
sheets and brush with beaten egg.

7 Using a plain 2.5 cm (1 inch)
round cutter, cut partway
through the centre of each round.

8 Bake in the oven at 220°C
(425°F) mark 7 for about 10
minutes. Remove the soft centres
from each bouchée and cool.

9 To serve, fill the cooled cases
with cold filling and reheat in
the oven at 180°C (350°F) mark 4
for about 5 minutes. Serve hot,
garnished with prawns and lemon.

Menu Suggestion
Bouchées (or 'little mouthfuls')
can be eaten with the fingers; just
right for a cocktail party.

RED CABBAGE SALAD

| 0.30 | f | 272 cals |

Serves 8

900 g (2 lb) red cabbage
150 ml (¼ pint) olive oil
150 ml (¼ pint) white wine vinegar
15 ml (1 tbsp) sugar
5 ml (1 tsp) paprika
60 ml (4 tbsp) redcurrant jelly
50 g (2 oz) Danish Blue
salt and freshly ground pepper
4 crisp dessert apples (eg Granny Smith's)

1 Shred the cabbage finely with a sharp knife, discarding any damaged outer leaves and thick, woody stalks.

2 Put the olive oil in a large bowl with the wine vinegar, sugar and paprika. Whisk vigorously with a fork until well combined. Heat the redcurrant jelly gently in a small saucepan until runny, then whisk into the dressing.

3 Crumble the cheese into the dressing, add salt and pepper to taste and whisk again.

4 Core the apples (but do not peel them). Slice them thinly, then place in a large salad bowl with the shredded cabbage. Pour over the dressing and toss well.

5 Cover the bowl tightly with cling film and chill in the refrigerator until serving time (up to 24 hours).

Menu Suggestion
Red Cabbage Salad is excellent served with any cold roast meat for buffet parties, and is also particularly good with hot roast pork and game—the sharpness of the dressing offsets the richness of the meat.

RED CABBAGE SALAD
The method used here of marinating red cabbage in oil and wine vinegar is a Danish one. The marinade has a softening as well as a flavouring effect on hard cabbage, so that the end result is almost as if the cabbage has been cooked. Called *rødkål* in Danish, red cabbage is traditionally served with cold pork, and with the Danish pork and beef meatballs called *frikadeller*.

HAM PINWHEELS

| 0.15* | £ | 15 cals |

* plus 2 hours chilling

Makes about 30 pinwheels

75 g (3 oz) full-fat soft cheese
10 ml (2 tsp) creamed horseradish
5 ml (1 tsp) finely chopped gherkins
salt and freshly ground pepper
113 g (4 oz) packet (5 thin slices)
lean ham
cucumber slices, to garnish

1 Mix the cheese, creamed horseradish and gherkins together and beat until soft. Add salt and pepper to taste.

2 On a flat surface, lay out the slices of ham. Spread the cheese mixture over the slices.

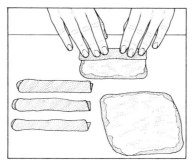

3 Roll up the slices like Swiss rolls. Put on a plate, seam side downwards, then cover with cling film. Chill in the refrigerator for at least 2 hours.

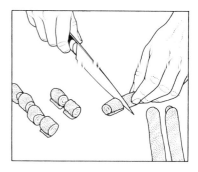

4 To serve, cut each roll into 2 cm ($\frac{3}{4}$ inch) thick slices with a sharp knife. Garnish with cucumber slices.

Menu Suggestion
Ham Pinwheels are just the thing to pass round at a Christmas drinks party. They look attractive on a large serving platter, and are easy to eat with the fingers.

HAM PINWHEELS

Just a teaspoon or two of horseradish can make all the difference to a filling, sauce or salad dressing. Horseradish is a perennial plant related to mustard; it has a powerfully hot bite to it, and should always be used in very small quantities. It is extremely easy to grow in the garden, and also easy to deal with at the harvesting stage. Simply lift the roots in the autumn, scrub them, then grate them into a jar and cover with wine vinegar. The creamed horseradish specified in this recipe is a commercially bottled condiment of grated horseradish mixed with vinegar, sugar, oil and cream. It is milder than grated horseradish.

CHEESE D'ARTOIS

| 0.45* £ ✳ | 60–80 cals |

* plus 30 minutes chilling

Makes 30–40

150 g (5 oz) Gruyère, grated

25 g (1 oz) walnut pieces, coarsely chopped

freshly ground pepper

1 egg, beaten

370 g (13 oz) packet frozen puff pastry, thawed

1 In a bowl, mix together the cheese, nuts and pepper to taste. Bind with the egg, reserving a little egg to glaze the pastry.

2 Roll out the pastry to a rectangle 40.5 × 38 cm (16 × 15 inches).

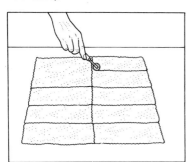

3 Cut the pastry into 10 strips, each measuring 20.5 × 7.5 cm (8 × 3 inches), using a pastry wheel for an attractive edge.

4 Lay 5 strips on an ungreased baking sheet, divide the filling equally between them and spread it out evenly, almost to the edges.

5 Cover with the remaining 5 strips and lightly press the edges to seal. Cover with cling film and chill in the refrigerator for 30 minutes.

6 Mark each strip into 6–8 fingers and brush with the reserved egg. Bake in the oven at 200°C (400°F) mark 6 for about 15 minutes until risen and golden brown. Cut the pastry through into fingers and serve immediately.

Menu Suggestion

Serve these nutty cheese fingers for cocktail 'nibbles' during the festive season, or at a Christmas party with a hot punch (page 143).

CHEESE D'ARTOIS

D'Artois or *Dartois* is a French pastry dish, made with either puff pastry as here, or with flaky pastry. Cheese is a popular filling, but there are also many French recipes for sweet *dartois*. French pastry cream (*crème pâtissière*) is used for the filling, sometimes flavoured with vanilla, ground almonds or rum. The method of making a pastry 'sandwich' then marking it into fingers, is always the same, for both the sweet and the savoury versions of *D'Artois*.

HOT CHEESE

| 0.15* | £ | ✳ | 53 cals |

* plus 1 hour chilling

Makes 24

~~1 rasher breaky bacon, rinded~~

100 g (4 oz) Cheddar, finely grated

50 g (2 oz) plain flour

50 g (2 oz) butter, softened

salt and freshly ground pepper

pinch of cayenne

15 ml (1 tbsp) caraway or sesame
  seeds

watercresss sprigs, to garnish
  (optional)

1 Grill the bacon until crisp,
then chop finely. Place in a
bowl with the other ingredients
and work together until they form
a ball.

2 Roll the mixture into 24 balls
and arrange on a large ungreased baking sheet. Cover with
cling film and chill in the
refrigerator for at least 1 hour
until firm.

3 To serve, uncover and bake in
the oven at 190°C (375°F)
mark 5 for about 10 minutes until
golden. Serve hot, garnished with
watercress sprigs if liked

Menu Suggestion
These tiny cheese and bacon
flavour balls make perfect finger
food for a drinks party when
guests are standing up. For even
easier eating, spear each ball on a
cocktail stick before arranging
them on a large platter.

CHEESE TWISTS

0.35* f ✳ 21 cals

* plus 30 minutes chilling
Makes about 70

| 65 g (2½ oz) butter, softened |
| 40 g (1½ oz) full-fat soft cheese |
| 1 egg yolk |
| 175 g (6 oz) plain flour |
| salt |
| cayenne |
| 30 ml (2 tbsp) freshly grated Parmesan |

1 In a bowl, beat the butter with the soft cheese and egg yolk. Sift in the flour with a pinch each of salt and cayenne, then stir until evenly mixed. Stir in 10 ml (2 tsp) water to form a dough.

2 Knead the dough lightly until smooth; wrap in cling film and chill for 30 minutes.

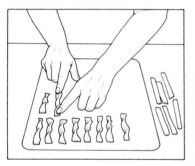

3 Roll out the pastry thinly and cut into narrow strips measuring about 7.5 cm × 5 mm (3 × ¼ inch). Twist the strips and place on ungreased baking sheets, pressing the ends down well to prevent the strips unwinding. Sprinkle with the Parmesan.

4 Bake in the oven at 180°C (350°F) mark 4 for about 15 minutes. Transfer to wire racks and leave to cool for about 15 minutes. Store in an airtight container for up to 2 weeks.

Menu Suggestion
Serve for a Christmas drinks party, on platters or in bowls.

VARIATIONS

MEDALLIONS
Prepare pastry, roll out and cut into 2.5 cm (1 inch) rounds. Sprinkle with Parmesan and bake. Cool. Either sandwich together or top the rounds with softened pâté, fish paste or cream cheese; garnish with slices of olives, radish or gherkin.

BLUE CHEESE STRAWS
Rub the butter into the flour with the seasonings. Grate 75 g (3 oz) blue cheese into the mixture, add the egg yolk and 2.5 ml (½ tsp) Dijon mustard. Mix to form a soft dough. Wrap and chill for 30 minutes and proceed from step 3.

SALTED ALMONDS OR HAZELNUTS

0.40* f f 2139 cals

* plus 30 minutes cooling
Makes 350 g (12 oz)

| 350 g (12 oz) shelled almonds or hazelnuts |
| 25 g (1 oz) butter or margarine |
| 10 ml (2 tsp) salt |

1 If the almonds are not blanched, put them in a bowl, cover with boiling water and leave for 3–4 minutes.

2 Drain the almonds, then plunge into cold water for 1 minute. Slide off the skins between your fingers.

3 To skin hazelnuts, put under a grill for 2–3 minutes, shaking the pan occasionally. Turn into a clean tea towel and rub off the skins.

4 Melt the butter in a roasting tin and add the almonds or hazelnuts, tossing them until they are evenly coated.

5 Roast in the oven at 150°C (300°F) mark 2 for 30 minutes, stirring occasionally. Add the salt and toss well. Cool for 30 minutes. Store in an airtight container for up to 2 weeks.

Menu Suggestion
Serve in bowls for a Christmas drinks party (see page 143 for Christmas drinks recipes).

VARIATIONS

CURRIED ALMONDS
Follow the recipe up to the beginning of step 4. Add 15 ml (1 tbsp) curry powder to the butter and continue to the end of the recipe. Use 5 ml (1 tsp) salt only.

SPICY PAPRIKA ALMONDS OR CASHEWS
Follow the recipe up to the beginning of step 4. Add 15 ml (1 tbsp) paprika and 2.5 ml (½ tsp) Chilli Seasoning to the butter and continue to the end of the recipe. Use 5 ml (1 tsp) salt only.

DANISH MUSHROOMS

| 0.15 | £ | 24 cals |

Makes about 20

225 g (8 oz) even-sized button
   mushrooms

150 ml ($\frac{1}{4}$ pint) soured cream

50 g (2 oz) jar black Danish-style
   caviar

parsley or dill sprigs, to garnish
   (optional)

1 Remove the stalks from the
   mushrooms and discard. Wipe
the mushroom caps with a clean,
damp cloth.

2 Divide the soured cream
   between the mushroom caps
and spoon a little Danish caviar
over each one. Garnish with tiny
parsley or dill sprigs, if liked.
Serve within 30 minutes.

Menu Suggestion
Arrange Danish Mushrooms on a
serving platter to hand round at a
cocktail party. Served on
individual plates, they also make a
most unusual starter for a dinner
party.

CRANBERRY CHEESECAKE

0.35*	£	477 cals

* plus 5 hours chilling and 30 minutes cooling

Serves 10

225 g (8 oz) full-fat soft cheese

2 eggs, separated

finely grated rind and juice of 2 lemons

225 g (8 oz) caster sugar

300 ml (½ pint) natural yogurt

300 ml (½ pint) double cream

15 ml (1 tbsp) gelatine

175 g (6 oz) wheatmeal (digestive) biscuits

75 g (3 oz) butter

225 g (8 oz) cranberries

10 ml (2 tsp) arrowroot

1 In a bowl, beat together cheese, egg yolks, lemon rind, 50 g (2 oz) of the sugar and the yogurt. Whip the cream lightly and fold into the cheese mixture.

2 In a small saucepan, heat 75 ml (5 tbsp) of lemon juice with 30 ml (2 tbsp) water. Sprinkle in the gelatine, stir briskly until dissolved. Stir into the cheese mixture and leave to cool.

3 Whisk the egg whites until standing in soft peaks, then fold into the cheese mixture until evenly incorporated.

4 Pour the mixture into a lightly oiled 25.5 cm (10 inch) fluted savarin spring form tin. Chill in the refrigerator for 3–4 hours until completely set.

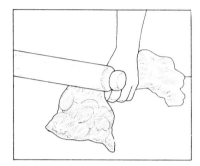

5 Put the biscuits in a polythene bag and crush with a rolling pin. Turn into a bowl.

6 Melt the butter in a small saucepan, then stir into the crushed biscuits.

7 Spoon the butter and biscuit mixture over the set cheese-cake and pat down firmly. Chill again for 1 hour until set.

8 Cook the cranberries, remaining sugar and 150 ml (¼ pint) water for about 10 minutes until soft but still whole. Blend a little water with the arrowroot, stir into the cranberry mixture and slowly bring to boiling point. Cook for 2–3 minutes then leave to cool for 30 minutes.

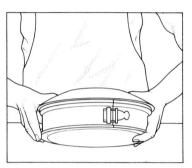

9 Invert the cheesecake on to a flat serving plate. Spoon the cranberry mixture into the centre before serving.

Menu Suggestion

Cranberry Cheesecake looks good as part of a buffet party spread. Serve with a jug of fresh pouring cream or soured cream, for those who like it.

CRANBERRY CHEESECAKE

The majority of the world's cranberries are harvested in North America. The name cranberry was given to the fruit by the Pilgrims in the 17th century, who thought the pink blossom of the cranberry looked like the heads of cranes. The nickname "crane berry" soon became shortened to cranberry, and in the early 19th century the Americans started cultivating the wild fruit on a large scale.

The North American Indians believed that this crimson red, tangy fruit had medicinal qualities, and the juice was used to draw poison out of arrow wounds. They also used the juice as a meat preservative, and as a natural dye for cloth.

PARTY PASSION PAVLOVA

| 1.30 | 🍳 | 299–374 cals |

Serves 8–10

4 egg whites
pinch of salt
275 g (10 oz) caster sugar
5 ml (1 tsp) vanilla flavouring
6.25 ml (1¼ tsp) cornflour
6.25 ml (1¼ tsp) vinegar
4 kiwi fruit
4 satsumas or mandarin oranges
few thin slices of preserved or
    stem ginger
60 ml (4 tbsp) whisky
30 ml (2 tbsp) ginger wine or syrup
    from the stem ginger
300 ml (½ pint) double or whipping
    cream
150 ml (¼ pint) thick, set yogurt or
    Quark
4 fresh passion fruit

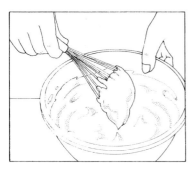

1 Put the egg whites in a large
bowl and whisk until stiff and
standing in peaks. Whisk in the
salt and 125 g (4 oz) of the sugar
until the meringue is glossy.

2 With a metal spoon, fold in
another 125 g (4 oz) of the
sugar with the vanilla flavouring,
cornflour and vinegar.

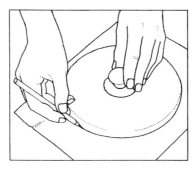

3 Draw a 25.5 cm (10 inch) circle
on a large sheet of non-stick
baking parchment. Place the
paper, marked side down, on a
baking sheet.

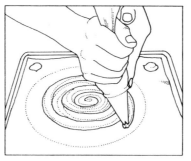

4 Spoon the meringue into a
large piping bag fitted with a
large plain nozzle. Pipe the
meringue in a spiral, starting at
the centre of the marked circle and
working outwards towards the
edge.

5 Pipe a second layer of
meringue on top of the outer
edge of the circle, to make a raised
lip to prevent the topping spilling
over the edge when serving.

6 Bake in the oven at 150°C
(300°F) mark 2 for 1 hour
until crisp and dry. With 2 fish
slices or wide metal spatulas, lift
the pavlova off the baking parchment and onto a wire rack. Leave
to cool.

7 Meanwhile, prepare the
topping. Peel the kiwi fruit
and slice thinly. Peel the satsumas
and divide into segments. Put the
preserved or stem ginger in a bowl
with the remaining sugar, the
whisky and ginger wine or syrup.
Add the prepared fruit and stir
gently to mix. Whip the cream
and yogurt together until thick.

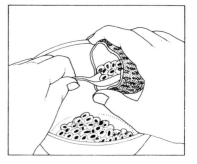

8 Just before serving, transfer
the cold pavlova to a large
serving platter. Spread the cream
mixture in the centre, then
arrange the fruit decoratively on
top. Pour over any juices. Slice the
passion fruit in half, scoop out the
flesh with a teaspoon, then
sprinkle over the top of the
pavlova. Serve within 1 hour or
the topping will make the pavlova
too soft.

Menu Suggestion
Pavlova is an impressive dessert
for a Christmas party. It needs no
accompaniment other than a
chilled dessert wine.

INDIVIDUAL APRICOT AND ORANGE SOUFFLÉS

| 1.30* | 🍴 | £ £ | ✳ | 334 cals |

* plus at least 4 hours chilling

Makes 6

a little vegetable oil, for brushing

3 eggs, separated

75 g (3 oz) caster sugar

15 ml (3 tsp) gelatine

finely grated rind and juice of 1 large orange

411 g (14½ oz) can apricot halves in syrup

60 ml (4 tbsp) orange-flavoured liqueur

150 ml (¼ pint) double cream

45 ml (3 tbsp) crushed ratafias or finely chopped almonds, and blanched orange shreds, to decorate

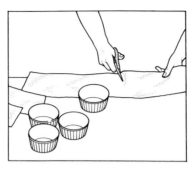

1 Cut strips of double grease-proof paper long enough to go round the outside of 6 individual soufflé dishes and 5 cm (2 inches) higher.

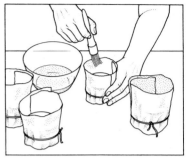

2 Tie the strips on the dishes securely with string and brush the inside of the paper lightly with a little vegetable oil.

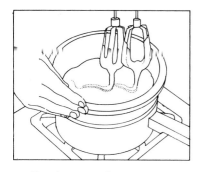

3 Put the egg yolks and sugar in a heatproof bowl standing over a pan of gently simmering water. Whisk until very thick and light and the beaters leave a ribbon trail when lifted.

4 Remove the bowl from the heat and continue whisking until cool.

5 In a saucepan, heat the orange juice. Take off the heat and sprinkle in the gelatine. Stir briskly until dissolved. Cool.

6 Meanwhile, work the apricots and their syrup in a blender or food processor (reserving 4 apricot halves for the decoration). Whisk the purée into the egg mixture with the orange rind and liqueur.

7 Whip the cream until it just holds its shape. In a separate bowl, whisk the egg whites until stiff and standing in peaks.

8 Stir the gelatine liquid into the egg yolk and sugar mixture, then fold in the cream followed by the egg whites. Pour slowly into the prepared dishes. Chill in the refrigerator for at least 4 hours, overnight if possible.

9 To serve, carefully remove the paper collars and brush a little oil around the exposed edge of the soufflé mixture.

10 Press the ratafias or nuts around the edge. Slice the reserved apricots and arrange decoratively on top of the soufflés with the orange shreds.

Menu Suggestion
Individual soufflés are a good idea for a buffet party because they make portion control and serving so easy. The apricot and orange flavour is very rich and creamy, so no accompaniment is necessary.

Puddings and Desserts

You should pull out all the stops for the dessert course at Christmastime. It's the one time in the year when just about everyone indulges in something sweet, even if they rarely do at other times during the course of the year. Christmas is a wonderful excuse for traditional trifles and plum puds, for boozy syllabubs and fruit salads, and extra special ice creams.

TRADITIONAL TRIFLE

| 1.00* | £ £ | 497–663 cals |

* plus 20 minutes infusing, 1 hour
cooling and 4–6 hours chilling

Serves 6–8

8 trifle sponges
175 g (6 oz) strawberry jam
100 g (4 oz) macaroons
200 ml (7 fl oz) medium sherry
568 ml (1 pint) milk
1 vanilla pod
2 whole eggs
2 egg yolks
15 ml (1 tbsp) cornflour
30 ml (2 tbsp) caster sugar
450 ml ($\frac{3}{4}$ pint) whipping cream
glacé cherries and angelica, or
    toasted flaked almonds,
    to decorate

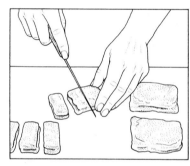

1 Split the trifle sponges in
half and spread with the jam.
Sandwich together and cut into
fingers. Arrange in the bottom of a
large, shallow glass serving dish.

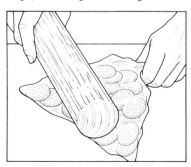

2 Crush the macaroons lightly
and sprinkle on top. Spoon
over the sherry and leave for 30
minutes to soak.

3 Meanwhile, put the milk and
vanilla pod in a saucepan,
bring to the boil, then remove
from the heat. Cover the pan and
leave to infuse for 20 minutes.

4 Put the eggs, egg yolks, cornflour and sugar in a heatproof
bowl standing over a saucepan of
gently simmering water (or in the
top of a double boiler). Add the
milk, removing the vanilla pod.
Place over gentle heat and cook
until the custard is thick enough to
coat the back of a wooden spoon,
stirring all the time.

5 Pour the custard over the
sponges. Leave for 1 hour
until cold, then chill in the
refrigerator for 3–4 hours.

6 Whip the cream until stiff.
Spread half on top of the
custard. Pipe the remaining cream
on top and decorate with the
cherries and angelica, or scatter
with almonds. Chill again for 1–2
hours before serving.

Menu Suggestion
Trifle is traditional in England
at teatime on Christmas Day, but
it can also be served as a dessert at
any time during the festive season.

TRADITIONAL TRIFLE
It seems we have to thank the
Victorians for giving us the trifle,
although they would probably
frown upon the elaborate fruit
and cream concoctions that call
themselves trifles these days.
The original Victorian trifle was
similar to this recipe, a bottom
layer of plain cake sandwiched
together with jam, a light
sprinkling of crushed macaroons,
and a heavy soaking of sherry!
This was then topped with a
vanilla-flavoured egg custard and
then a final layer of whipped
cream. Cherries, angelica and
almonds were the traditional
trifle decoration.

SUGAR-FREE CHRISTMAS PUDDING

$\boxed{0.20^*}$ f $\boxed{273 \text{ cals}}$

* plus 4 hours steaming, 1 month
maturing and 2 hours reheating

Serves 6

225 g (8 oz) mixed dried fruit

juice of 2 oranges

150 ml ($\frac{1}{4}$ pint) brandy

1 large carrot, grated

1 large apple, grated

50 g (2 oz) plain wholemeal flour

50 g (2 oz) fresh wholemeal
   breadcrumbs

25 g (1 oz) blanched almonds,
   chopped

5 ml (1 tsp) grated nutmeg

5 ml (1 tsp) ground cinnamon

2 eggs, beaten

holly sprig, to decorate

1 Put the mixed dried fruit in a
large bowl. Stir in the orange
juice and the brandy. Cover and
leave overnight. Add all the
remaining ingredients and mix
well together.

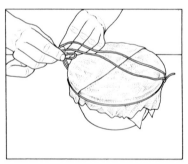

2 Grease a 900 ml (1$\frac{1}{2}$ pint)
pudding basin and fill with the
mixture. Cover with a piece of
pleated greaseproof paper and
then foil. Secure tightly with
string, making a handle for easy
lifting in and out of pan.

3 Place the basin in a steamer or
over a saucepan filled with
boiling water to come halfway up
the sides of the basin. Steam over
boiling water for about 4 hours,
topping up with boiling water as
necessary.

4 When cooked, remove the
pudding from the pan and
leave to cool for at least 2 hours.
Unwrap, then rewrap in fresh
greaseproof paper and foil.

5 Store in a cool, dry place to
mature for at least 1 month.
To serve, steam for a further 2
hours. Turn out onto a warmed
plate and decorate with holly.

Menu Suggestion
This is the perfect pud for the diet
conscious. The combination of
grated carrot and fruit is quite
sweet enough without additional
sugar, and the absence of suet also
helps to make it a 'healthy' recipe.

VACHERIN AU CHOCOLAT ET AUX MARRONS
(CHOCOLATE AND CHESTNUT MERINGUE GÂTEAU)

2.00* 🍮 🍮	468–561 cals

* plus cooling and chilling

Serves 10–12

175 g (6 oz) shelled hazelnuts

6 egg whites

350 g (12 oz) caster sugar

225 g (8 oz) dark or bitter chocolate

60 ml (4 tbsp) dark rum

350 g (12 oz) sweetened chestnut
   purée (from a can or tube)

300 ml (½ pint) double or whipping
   cream

chocolate caraque or grated
   chocolate, to decorate

1 Grease and base-line three
20.5 cm (8 inch) sandwich tins.

2 Toast the hazelnuts lightly
under the grill, shaking the
pan frequently.

3 Transfer the nuts to a clean
tea-towel and rub gently while
still hot to remove the skins.
Grind until very fine.

4 Put the egg whites in a large
bowl and beat until very stiff
and standing in peaks. Beat in half
of the sugar until the meringue is
glossy. Fold in the remaining
sugar with the hazelnuts.

5 Spoon the meringue into the
prepared sandwich tins. Level
the tops and bake in the oven at
180°C (350°F) mark 4 for 35–40
minutes until crisp.

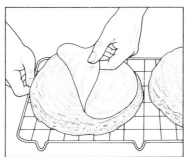

6 Invert the tins onto a wire rack
and turn out the meringues.
Peel off the lining papers carefully. (Do not worry if the
meringues are cracked, this will
not show in the finished dessert.)
Leave to cool.

7 Break the chocolate in pieces
into a heatproof bowl standing
over a saucepan of gently
simmering water. Add the rum
and heat gently until the chocolate
has melted, stirring only once or
twice after the chocolate has
started to melt. Remove from the
heat and gradually blend in 225 g
(8 oz) of the chestnut purée.

8 Put 1 meringue round, soft
side uppermost, on a serving
plate. Spread with half of the
chocolate and chestnut mixture,
then top with the second meringue
round, crisp side uppermost.
Spread with the remaining mixture
then top with the last round.

9 Whip the cream until it holds
its shape. Reserve 30 ml
(2 tbsp) of the cream and swirl the
remainder all over the gâteau to
cover the top and sides completely.
Blend the remaining chestnut
purée into the reserved cream,
then pipe around the edge.
Decorate with chocolate. Chill in
the refrigerator.

Menu Suggestion
This gâteau is very special, and
best reserved for occasions when
you want to impress.

TANGERINE SYLLABUB

1.00* ☐ £ £ 335 cals

* plus 2 hours macerating and 2 hours chilling

Serves 6

700 g (1½ lb) tangerines—about 6

30 ml (2 tbsp) lemon juice

30 ml (2 tbsp) orange-flavoured liqueur

50 g (2 oz) dark soft brown sugar

300 ml (½ pint) double cream

sponge fingers, to serve

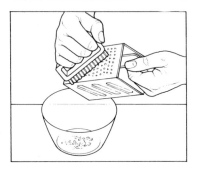

1 Finely grate the rind from 3 tangerines into a small bowl; use a stiff brush to remove all the rind from the teeth of the grater.

2 Peel these 3 tangerines and pull the segments apart. Remove the membranes from around each segment if tough.

3 Halve and squeeze the remaining tangerines, or liquidise the flesh and strain it.

4 Measure out 120 ml (8 tbsp) juice. Strain over the tangerine rinds. Add the lemon juice and liqueur, then cover and leave to soak for at least 2 hours.

5 Put the sugar in a bowl and strain in the liquid. Mix well until the sugar has dissolved.

6 Whip the cream until stiff, then gradually whisk in the juices, keeping the cream thick.

7 Put the tangerine segments in the base of 6 stemmed glasses, reserving 6 segments for decoration. Divide the cream mixture between the glasses, cover with cling film and chill in the refrigerator for 2 hours.

8 Decorate with tangerine segments and serve with sponge fingers.

TANGERINE SYLLABUB

The syllabub is one of the oldest of English desserts. Originally it was made with very fresh milk—wine was poured into a bowl, then the cow milked straight into it! The idea behind this was that the acid in the wine curdled the warm milk. Early 19th century recipes for syllabub suggested that the milk should be poured from a height onto the alcohol, in the absence of a cow ready for milking. These days, fresh double cream is used, with equal success!

Menu Suggestion

Tangerine Syllabub is rich and creamy. Serve for a Christmas dessert after a plain roast main course such as Roast Rib of Beef with Batter Pudding (page 37).

GRAPE SORBET

0.30* ☐ £ ✳ 221 cals

* plus 6–7 hours freezing

Serves 6

900 g (2 lb) black grapes

125 g (4 oz) granulated sugar

10 ml (2 tsp) lemon juice

1 egg white

45 ml (3 tbsp) kirsch

brandy snaps, to serve

1 Pluck the grapes off the stalks but do not bother to peel or seed them.

2 Put the sugar in a heavy-based saucepan with 450 ml (¾ pint) water and heat gently until the sugar has dissolved. Bring to the boil and bubble for 5 minutes. Remove from the heat, stir in the lemon juice, then cool slightly.

3 Put the grapes and sugar syrup together in a blender or food processor and work to a purée. Sieve to remove the seeds and skin.

4 Pour into a shallow freezer container and freeze for 4–5 hours or until the mixture is beginning to set. Remove the sorbet from the freezer and mash with a fork to break down the ice crystals.

5 Whisk the egg white lightly, then fold the kirsch and egg white into the sorbet. Return to the freezer and freeze for at least a further 2 hours until firm.

6 Serve the grape sorbet straight from the freezer, with brandy snaps handed separately.

Menu Suggestion

Grape Sorbet is tangy and refreshing. It makes the perfect alternative dessert to Christmas pudding for those who prefer something less heavy.

THREE FRUIT SALAD

0.50*	£	95 cals

* plus chilling

Serves 8

50 g (2 oz) granulated sugar
15 ml (1 tbsp) lemon juice
15 ml (1 tbsp) kirsch
1 pineapple, weighing about 1.1 kg
  (2½ lb)
225 g (8 oz) black grapes
4 fresh kiwi fruit

1 Put the sugar in a heavy-based saucepan with 150 ml (¼ pint) water. Heat gently until the sugar has dissolved, then bring to the boil and bubble for 2 minutes. Remove from the heat, stir in the lemon juice and kirsch, then set aside to cool.

2 Prepare the pineapple. With a sharp knife, cut off the leafy top and discard. Cut the pineapple into 1 cm (½ inch) pieces. Cut off the skin and dig out the 'eyes' with the tip of the knife. Cut out the core from each slice with an apple corer or small biscuit cutter. Cut the flesh into chunks.

3 Wash and dry the grapes, then halve. Remove the pips by flicking them out with the point of a sharp knife.

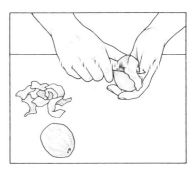

4 Peel the kiwi fruit using a potato peeler or sharp knife, then slice the flesh thinly.

5 Stir the prepared fruits into the syrup, cover and chill well in the refrigerator before serving.

Menu Suggestion
Offer this refreshingly light fruit salad as an alternative to the traditional plum pudding on Christmas Day. It can be prepared the day beforehand and kept in the refrigerator overnight. Serve with fresh pouring cream.

THREE FRUIT SALAD
Kiwi fruit are sometimes also called Chinese gooseberries, from the fact that they originated in China, and have hairy skin like a gooseberry. The name kiwi fruit is more common nowadays, however, after the national bird of New Zealand, where the fruit was first cultivated on a large scale. Now they have become so popular that they are grown all over the world, as much for their attractive appearance when used as a decoration for both sweet and savoury dishes, as for their unique, sweet flavour and juicy flesh.

ICED TUTTI FRUTTI PUDDING

0.30* 🔲 £ £ ✳ 624 cals

* plus 2–3 hours soaking fruit, 6–7 hours freezing and 20 minutes standing before serving

Serves 8

100 g (4 oz) glacé cherries

40 g (1½ oz) angelica

50 g (2 oz) blanched almonds

4 canned pineapple rings, drained

120 ml (8 tbsp) orange-flavoured liqueur

900 ml (1½ pints) whipping cream

130 g (4½ oz) caster sugar

6 eggs, beaten

1 Cut the cherries in half, finely chop the angelica, almonds and roughly chop the pineapple.

2 Pour over the liqueur, cover and leave to macerate for 2–3 hours, stirring occasionally.

3 Meanwhile, put the cream, sugar and eggs in a heatproof bowl standing over a saucepan of gently simmering water (or in the top of a double boiler). Place over gentle heat and cook until the custard is thick enough to coat the back of a wooden spoon, stirring all the time. Do not boil.

4 Pour the custard into a large bowl, cover and leave to cool for about 1 hour. When cold, freeze the custard for about 2 hours until mushy in texture.

5 Mash the frozen mixture with a fork, then freeze again for about 2 hours until slushy.

6 Mash the frozen mixture again and stir in the fruit mixture. Mix well and pack into a 1.4 litre (2½ pint) pudding basin, base-lined with non-stick paper. Return to freezer for 2–3 hours until firm.

7 About 1 hour before serving, remove from the freezer and leave to soften slightly at room temperature. Turn out and serve immediately.

Menu Suggestion

This dessert is like an ice cream version of Christmas pudding. Serve it instead of Christmas pudding for a change—children usually prefer it to the rich and heavy traditional plum pudding.

ICED TUTTI FRUTTI PUDDING

Tutti frutti, which literally translated means 'all fruit' in Italian, was originally an American invention. Assorted fruits such as cherries, currants, raspberries, strawberries, apricots, peaches and pineapple were steeped in brandy in a stone crock for at least 3 months.

RASPBERRY REDCURRANT FREEZE

| 0.30* | ✳ | 284–392 cals |

* plus 1 hour chilling, 4 hours freezing
and 1 hour standing before serving

Serves 4–6

**350 g (12 oz) fresh or frozen
    raspberries**

225 g (8 oz) jar redcurrant jelly

300 ml (½ pint) soured cream

small crisp biscuits, to serve

1 Put the raspberries and jelly in
a saucepan and heat gently,
stirring frequently, until the fruit
is soft. Transfer to a blender or
food processor and work to a
purée. Sieve to remove the seeds.
Chill in the refrigerator for about
1 hour until cold.

2 Whisk in the soured cream,
then pour into a freezer container (not metal) at least 5 cm
(2 inches) deep. Freeze for about 2
hours until firm but not hard.

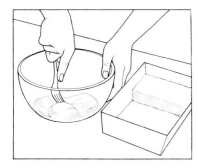

3 Turn the frozen mixture into a
bowl and break into pieces.
Beat until smooth, creamy and
lighter in colour. Return to the
freezer container and freeze for a
further 2 hours until firm.

4 Allow to soften slightly in the
refrigerator for about 1 hour
before serving with biscuits.

Menu Suggestion
Serve for a cool and refreshing
dessert after a rich main course.

Christmas Baking

Baking at Christmastime is a real pleasure. All the traditional favourites can be made, and you have a wonderful excuse to go to town on the decoration. This chapter is packed with ideas from all round the world, some old, some new, but each one a winner.

CHRISTMAS CAKE

2.75–3.15* ⏣ £ £ 410 cals

* plus overnight macerating; make cake at least 1 month in time required; icing times vary — see pages 140–141 for decorating details

Serves about 25

225 g (8 oz) glacé cherries
575 g (1 lb 4 oz) mixed dried fruit
60 ml (4 tbsp) brandy
350 g (12 oz) plain flour
15 ml (3 tsp) baking powder
2.5 ml ($\frac{1}{2}$ tsp) salt
50 g (2 oz) chopped almonds
200 g (7 oz) soft brown sugar
200 ml (7 fl oz) corn oil
3 eggs
75–90 ml (5–6 tbsp) milk
150 ml ($\frac{1}{4}$ pint) apricot glaze, to decorate (page 140)
450 g (1 lb) almond paste (page 140)
royal icing made with 450 g (1 lb) icing sugar, to decorate (page 141)

1 Grease and line a deep 20.5 cm (8 inch) round cake tin with greaseproof paper.

2 Cut each cherry in half and place in a bowl. Add the dried fruit and brandy and mix together. Cover and leave to macerate overnight.

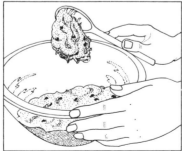

3 The next day, place the next 7 ingredients in a separate bowl. Add 60 ml (4 tbsp) of the milk and beat until well blended. Fold in the fruit with more milk to give a soft dropping consistency.

4 Turn into the prepared tin and bake in the oven at 170°C (325°F) mark 3 for 1 hour. Lower the oven temperature to 150°C (300°F) mark 2 and bake for a further $1\frac{1}{4}$–$1\frac{1}{2}$ hours, covering with double greaseproof paper, to avoid overbrowning, if necessary. The cake is cooked when a fine warmed skewer inserted in the centre comes out clean.

5 When the cake is cooked, leave to cool in the tin for 30 minutes, then turn out on to a wire rack and leave to cool completely.

6 To store, wrap the cake in several layers of greaseproof paper, then in foil. Store in an airtight tin for at least 1 month to mature before decorating.

Menu Suggestion
Home-made Christmas cake is a must at Christmas time, not only for tea on Christmas Day, but also for those occasions when people drop in for a drink.

CHRISTMAS CAKE

This recipe for Christmas cake gives a beautifully moist, dark result. Like all rich fruit cakes, it improves with keeping. If well wrapped and stored in an airtight tin, it will keep fresh for up to a year. One way of improving both the flavour and the moistness of the cake is to unwrap the cake, prick the top with a fine skewer and sprinkle over 15–30 ml (1–2 tbsp) brandy, rum or sherry. Wrap the cake again in greaseproof, then in foil, and return to the cake tin, which must be airtight. If you are storing the cake for several months, this can be done every month or so, if you are storing it for a shorter time, the soaking process can be repeated once every two or three weeks.

ALMOND SPONGE CHRISTMAS CAKE WITH GLACÉ FRUIT

2.30* 🍴🍴	477–597 cals

* plus cooling

Serves 8–10

225 g (8 oz) butter or margarine

225 g (8 oz) caster sugar

4 eggs, beaten

125 g (4 oz) self-raising flour, sifted
  with a pinch of salt

100 g (4 oz) ground almonds

225 g (8 oz) can pineapple slices

about 30 ml (2 tbsp) warm water

30 ml (2 tbsp) apricot jam

50 g (2 oz) glacé cherries

50 g (2 oz) blanched almonds

25–40 g (1–1½ oz) candied angelica

red and green ribbon, to decorate

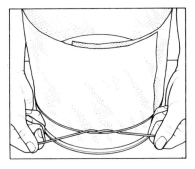

1 Prepare the cake tin. Grease and base line a deep 20.5 cm (8 inch) loose-bottomed round cake tin. Tie a double thickness of brown paper around the outside of the tin, to come about 5 cm (2 inches) above the rim.

2 Put the butter and sugar in a large bowl and beat until light and fluffy. Add the eggs a little at a time and beat until thoroughly combined. Add a little of the flour with the last addition of the egg, to prevent curdling, then beat in the ground almonds and the remaining flour.

3 Drain the pineapple slices and chop roughly. Dry thoroughly with absorbent kitchen paper. Fold into the cake mixture, then add enough warm water to give a soft dropping consistency. Spoon the mixture into the prepared cake tin and level the surface.

4 Bake the cake in the oven at 170°C (325°F) mark 3 for 1½ hours or until cooked through, covering the top with a double thickness of greaseproof paper after 1 hour's cooking time, if necessary, to prevent over-browning. To test if the cake is cooked, insert a warmed fine skewer in the centre—it should come out clean.

5 Leave the cake to settle in the tin for 5–10 minutes, then remove and stand on a wire rack.

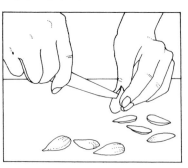

6 Make the decoration for the top of the cake while the cake is still warm. Cut the glacé cherries in half. Split the blanched almonds in half lengthways. Cut the angelica into diamond shapes.

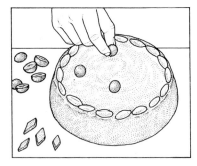

7 Warm half of the jam until melted, then sieve and brush over the top of the warm cake. Press the cherries, nuts and angelica on top of the cake in a decorative design (as in the photograph or use your own design). Melt and sieve the remaining jam, then brush over the design.

8 To serve, tie red and green ribbon around the cake to give it a festive look. Store the cake in an airtight tin for up to 2 weeks.

Menu Suggestion
This cake is equally good served at teatime or with morning coffee.

ALMOND SPONGE CHRISTMAS CAKE WITH GLACÉ FRUIT

For those who do not like the traditional rich fruit cake at Christmas, this cake is the perfect alternative. The cake itself is light and moist, and the decoration looks as festive as a traditional snowscene, or any other design using marzipan and royal icing.

  The decoration of glacé cherries, almonds and candied angelica gives a Christmassy look, but you can vary this according to taste; at Christmas-time, many stores and delicatessens stock other glacé fruit such as apricots and pineapples.

SWEDISH GINGER CAKE

1.45* £ ✳ 292 cals

* plus about 1¼ hours cooling

Serves about 10

100 g (4 oz) butter or block margarine
175 g (6 oz) caster sugar
3 eggs, beaten
200 g (7 oz) plain flour
5 ml (1 tsp) bicarbonate of soda
7.5 ml (1½ tsp) ground ginger
5 ml (1 tsp) ground mixed spice
150 ml (¼ pint) soured cream
25 g (1 oz) stem ginger, chopped
15 ml (1 tbsp) stem ginger syrup
15 ml (1 tbsp) black treacle
butter, to serve

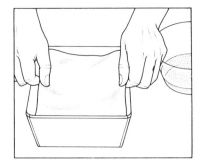

1 Grease and base line an 18 cm (7 inch) square cake tin with greased greaseproof paper.

2 Put the butter in a bowl and beat until soft. Gradually add the sugar and beat until fluffy.

3 Add the eggs, a little at a time, beating well after each addition until thoroughly incorporated.

4 Sift together the flour, bicarbonate of soda, ground ginger and mixed spice. Fold half into the creamed mixture.

5 Add the soured cream, stem ginger and syrup, black treacle and remaining flour. Fold in until well mixed.

6 Spoon the mixture into the prepared tin. Bake in the oven at 170°C (325°F) mark 3 for about 1¼ hours until the centre is firm to the touch.

7 Leave the cake to cool in the tin for about 15 minutes, then turn out on to a wire rack and leave to cool completely. Store in an airtight container for up to 2 weeks. Serve with butter.

Menu Suggestion
Swedish Ginger Cake is moist, dark and spicy. Serve it with coffee and sherry when visitors call during the festive season.

STOLLEN
(GERMAN YEAST CAKE WITH DRIED FRUIT)

2.00* | 145–218 cals

* plus 1–2 hours cooling

Serves 8–12

15 g ($\frac{1}{2}$ oz) fresh yeast or 7.5 ml
   (1$\frac{1}{2}$ tsp) dried yeast plus a pinch
   of sugar

100 ml (4 fl oz) tepid milk

225 g (8 oz) strong plain flour

1.25 ml ($\frac{1}{4}$ tsp) salt

25 g (1 oz) block margarine

grated rind of 1 small lemon

50 g (2 oz) chopped mixed peel

50 g (2 oz) currants

50 g (2 oz) sultanas

25 g (1 oz) blanched almonds,
   chopped

$\frac{1}{2}$ a beaten egg

icing sugar, to dredge

1 Grease a large baking sheet.
Crumble the fresh yeast into a
bowl and cream with the milk
until smooth. If using the dried
yeast and sugar, sprinkle the mixture into the milk and leave in a
warm place for 15 minutes until
the surface is frothy.

2 Put the flour and salt into a
bowl and rub in the margarine.
Add the lemon rind, fruit and
nuts. Add the yeast mixture and
beaten egg and mix to a soft dough.

3 Turn on to a lightly floured
working surface and knead for
about 10 minutes until smooth.

4 Cover with a clean cloth and
leave to rise in a warm place
for about 1 hour until doubled.

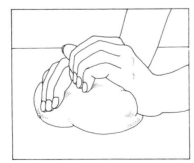

5 Knead the dough for 2–3
minutes, then roll into an oval
shape about 23 × 18 cm (9 × 7
inches). Mark a line lengthways
with the rolling pin.

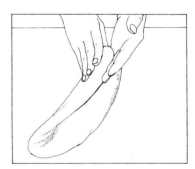

6 Carefully fold the dough in
half along the marked line.
Place on the baking sheet, cover
with a clean cloth and leave in a
warm place for about 40 minutes
until doubled in size.

7 Bake in the oven at 200°C
(400°F) mark 6 for about 30
minutes until well risen and
golden brown. Transfer to a wire
rack to cool. To serve, dredge all
over with icing sugar. Store in an
airtight tin for up to 3 days.

Menu Suggestion
In Germany, Stollen is eaten
throughout the Christmas period,
with afternoon coffee at 4 o'clock.

BLACK BUN

4.00* ⬜ £ £ 612 cals

* plus 1–2 hours cooling

Serves 12

450 g (1 lb) plain flour

pinch of salt

50 g (2 oz) butter or margarine

50 g (2 oz) lard

5 ml (1 tsp) ground cinnamon

5 ml (1 tsp) ground ginger

5 ml (1 tsp) ground allspice

5 ml (1 tsp) cream of tartar

5 ml (1 tsp) bicarbonate of soda

450 g (1 lb) seedless raisins

450 g (1 lb) currants

50 g (2 oz) chopped mixed peel

100 g (4 oz) chopped almonds

100 g (4 oz) dark soft brown sugar

1 egg, beaten

150 ml ($\frac{1}{4}$ pint) whisky

about 60 ml (4 tbsp) milk

beaten egg, to glaze

1 Put 225 g (8 oz) of the flour and the salt in a bowl. Add the butter and lard and rub in until the mixture resembles bread-crumbs. Add 30–45 ml (2–3 tbsp) cold water and stir until mixture begins to stick together. Knead lightly for a few seconds to give a firm, smooth dough.

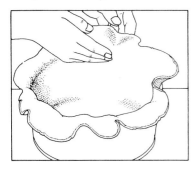

2 Grease a deep 20.5 cm (8 inch) round cake tin. Roll out two-thirds of the dough on a lightly floured working surface into a round about 35 cm (14 inches) in diameter. Line the prepared tin with the pastry, making sure it overhangs the sides. Refrigerate while preparing the filling.

3 Sift together the remaining flour, the spices, cream of tartar and bicarbonate of soda. Mix in the raisins, currants, peel, almonds and sugar.

4 Add the egg, whisky and milk and stir until the mixture is evenly moistened. Pack the filling into the pastry case and fold the top of the pastry over.

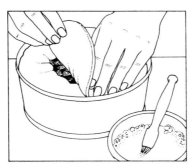

5 On a lightly floured surface, roll out the remaining dough to a 20.5 cm (8 inch) round. Moisten the edges of the pastry case, put the pastry round on top and seal the edges firmly together.

6 With a skewer, make four or five holes right down to the bottom of the cake, then prick all over the top with a fork and brush with beaten egg.

7 Bake in the oven at 180°C (350°F) mark 4 for 2½–3 hours or until a warmed fine skewer inserted in the centre comes out clean. Check near the end of cook-ing time and cover with several layers of greaseproof paper, if it is overbrowning. Turn out on to a wire rack and leave for 1–2 hours to cool completely, before serving.

Menu Suggestion

To enjoy this deliciously rich cake at its best, it should be made up to 1 month before you plan to serve it. Keep it stored in an airtight tin.

BLACK BUN

This traditional cake is also called Scotch Bun. In Scotland, it is served with glasses of whisky on New Year's Eve. Tradition has it that just at the moment when the clock strikes twelve, Black Bun and tots of whisky are brought out to welcome the first visitors or 'first footers' of the New Year. Shortbread (page 117) is also traditionally served at this time.

In Scotland, recipes for Black Bun vary from one region to another, but the things they all have in common are a large quantity of dried fruit, spices, whisky and a pastry crust. Some versions are made entirely without fat.

All Black Buns improve with keeping, and are best left to mature for at least 1 month before cutting. Many Scottish cooks wouldn't dream of cutting Black Bun until it has matured for a full 12 months.

GINGERBREAD HOUSE

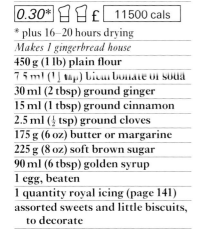

0.30* 🗍 🗍 £ | 11500 cals

* plus 16–20 hours drying

Makes 1 gingerbread house

450 g (1 lb) plain flour
7.5 ml (1½ tsp) bicarbonate of soda
30 ml (2 tbsp) ground ginger
15 ml (1 tbsp) ground cinnamon
2.5 ml (½ tsp) ground cloves
175 g (6 oz) butter or margarine
225 g (8 oz) soft brown sugar
90 ml (6 tbsp) golden syrup
1 egg, beaten
1 quantity royal icing (page 141)
assorted sweets and little biscuits, to decorate

1 Cut out templates for the house according to the diagram, using greaseproof paper or cardboard. Line 2 baking sheets with non-stick baking parchment.

2 Sift the flour, bicarbonate of soda and spices into a bowl. Rub in the butter with your fingertips until the mixture resembles fine breadcrumbs. Add the sugar and mix well.

3 Put the syrup in a warm basin and beat in the egg. Stir this mixture into the flour. Mix together to form a soft dough and knead until smooth. Cut in half and wrap one half in cling film.

4 On a lightly floured surface, roll out the other half of the dough to 0.5 cm (¼ inch) thickness. Using the templates, cut out one of each shape with a sharp knife, and carefully transfer to the pre-pared baking sheets. Cut out windows and a front door, if liked. Straighten the edges and chill in the refrigerator for 15 minutes.

5 Bake in the oven at 190°C (375°F) mark 5 for 8–10 minutes until golden brown. Leave to cool on the baking sheet for 5 minutes, then transfer to a wire rack and cool completely.

6 Knead the trimmings together with the remaining ginger-bread dough and roll out as before. Cut out one of each of the shapes, transfer to the lined baking sheet and bake as before.

7 Using the royal icing, sweets and biscuits, decorate the flat walls, windows and doors. Allow to dry for about 4–6 hours.

8 Assemble the house by cementing the four walls together with royal icing and securing to a 25.5 cm (10 inch) square cake board. Allow to dry for 4–6 hours. Stick the chimney pieces together and allow to dry.

9 If liked, fill the inside of the house with sweets. Using more royal icing, cement the roof pieces to the house and add the chimney. Allow to dry for 4–6 hours.

10 Cover the roof and chimney with royal icing, forking up to resemble snow and icicles, adding extra to the windows, if liked. Press sweets lightly into the icing to decorate the roof and walls. Spread more icing over the cake board and decorate with more sweets, or dust with icing sugar to resemble snow. Dry for at least 8 hours. Eat within 2 days.

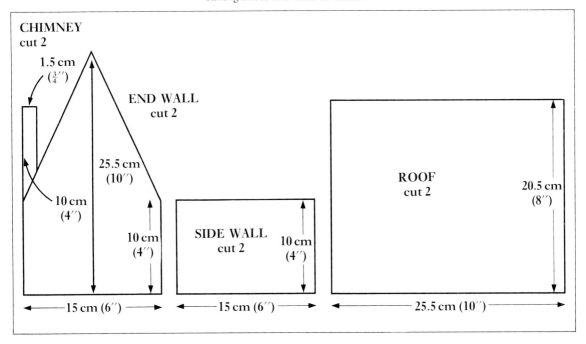

WALNUT AND COFFEE LAYER CAKE

1.15* ▯ ▯ £ **352–470 cals**

* plus 30 minutes cooling

Serves 6–8

4 egg yolks

350 g (12 oz) caster sugar, plus a
little extra for dredging

75 g (3 oz) walnuts, finely chopped

25 g (1 oz) fresh brown
breadcrumbs

25 g (1 oz) plain flour, plus a
little extra for dredging

5 egg whites

40 g (1½ oz) butter

75 g (3 oz) icing sugar

10 ml (2 tsp) coffee flavouring

pinch of cream of tartar

walnut halves, to decorate

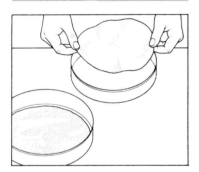

1 Grease and line two 18 cm
(7 inch) sandwich tins. Dredge
with the extra caster sugar and
flour, knocking out any excess.

2 Put the egg yolks and 125 g
(4 oz) of the measured caster
sugar in a bowl and whisk together
until very pale. Fold in the
walnuts, breadcrumbs and the
measured flour.

3 In a separate bowl, whisk 4 of
the egg whites until stiff but
not dry. Stir 1 large spoonful into
the egg yolk mixture to loosen it,
then fold in the remainder.

4 Divide the mixture between
the prepared sandwich tins.
Level the surface. Bake in the
oven at 180°C (350°F) mark 4 for
about 30 minutes until risen and
firm to the touch. Turn out on to a
wire rack and leave to cool for 30
minutes.

5 Make the filling. Put the
butter in a bowl and beat until
soft. Sift in the icing sugar and
beat well, adding the coffee
flavouring. Use to sandwich the 2
cakes together.

6 Make the frosting. Whisk the
remaining egg white until stiff.
Put the remaining caster sugar in a
saucepan with 60 ml (4 tbsp) water
and the cream of tartar and heat
gently, stirring, until dissolved.
Then, without stirring, boil to
120°C (240°F) on a sugar
thermometer.

7 Remove the syrup from the
heat and immediately the
bubbles subside, pour it onto the
egg white in a thin stream,
whisking the mixture continuously
to make a frosting.

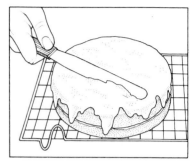

8 When the frosting thickens,
shows signs of going dull
around the edges and is almost
cold, pour it over the cake and
spread evenly with a palette knife.
Decorate at once with the walnut
halves. Leave to set before
serving. Store in an airtight container for up to 2–3 days.

Menu Suggestion
Serve this delicious layer cake to
Christmas guests with morning
coffee. It is very rich, so keep
portions small.

**WALNUT AND COFFEE
LAYER CAKE**

This is a traditional American
cake. Layers of superlight
sponge sandwiched together with
a luscious butter cream and
covered in a fluffy, snow-white
frosting.

If you are unfamiliar with
American frosting, don't be
daunted by the prospect of
making a sugar syrup with a
thermometer. It is not at all
difficult to make, and you are
bound to find the end result
so spectacular that you will think
your efforts have been well
worthwhile.

PANETTONE
(ITALIAN YEAST CAKE WITH CANDIED PEEL)

1.30*	🍰 🍰	290 cals

* plus rising, proving and cooling

Serves 10

350 g (12 oz) plain white flour

20 g ($\frac{3}{4}$ oz) fresh yeast or 15 g ($2\frac{1}{4}$ tsp) dried

225 ml (8 fl oz) tepid milk

100 g (4 oz) butter, softened

3 egg yolks

50 g (2 oz) caster sugar

75 g (3 oz) candied peel, chopped

50 g (2 oz) sultanas

pinch of grated nutmeg

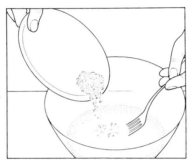

1 Prepare the dough. Sift the flour into a large bowl and make a well in the centre. Blend the fresh yeast with the milk. If using dried yeast, sprinkle it into the milk and leave in a warm place for 15 minutes until frothy. Add the yeast liquid to the flour and mix well together, gradually drawing in the flour from the sides of the bowl. Leave to stand in a warm place for 45 minutes or until doubled in bulk.

2 Add the softened butter to the dough with 2 of the egg yolks, the sugar, candied peel, sultanas and nutmeg. Mix well together. Leave to stand again in a warm place for a further 45 minutes or until doubled in bulk.

3 Meanwhile, cut 3 strips of baking parchment, each one measuring 56 × 25.5 cm (22 × 10 inches). Fold each piece over lengthways.

4 Stand the 3 pieces of parchment together on a greased baking sheet to make a 17 cm (6$\frac{1}{2}$ inch) circle and secure with staples. Place the dough inside the paper and leave in a warm place for about 1 hour or until risen to the top of the paper.

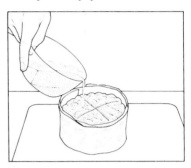

5 Cut the top of the dough in the shape of a cross, then pour over the last egg yolk. Bake on the lowest shelf of the oven at 200°C (400°F) mark 6 for 20 minutes, then lower the temperature to 180°C (350°F) mark 4 for a further 40 minutes or until a skewer inserted in the centre comes out clean. Leave to cool in the paper, then store in an airtight tin for a maximum of 1 week.

Menu Suggestion
In Milan, Panettone is traditionally served with sparkling white wine after lunch on Christmas Day, and at midnight on New Year's Eve.

PANETTONE
Panettone comes from Milan in northern Italy. The cakes are exported in attractive tall boxes, which can be seen hanging in Italian delicatessens all over the world. Panettone made at home is not so tall as the commercial varieties, and its texture is not quite so open, but it makes a deliciously light alternative to heavy Christmas fruit cakes.

BÛCHE DE NOËL
(FRENCH CHRISTMAS LOG)

2.00* ☐ £ £ ✳*

759–1012 cals

* plus 35 minutes cooling; freeze after step 8

Serves 6–8

1 egg white

175 g (6 oz) caster sugar, plus a little extra for dredging

3 eggs, size 2

75 g (3 oz) plain flour, plus a little extra for dredging

30 ml (2 tbsp) cocoa powder

225 g (8 oz) unsalted butter

50 g (2 oz) plain chocolate

500 g (1 lb) icing sugar, plus a little extra for decorating

440 g (15½ oz) can sweetened chestnut purée

holly sprigs, to decorate

1 Line a baking sheet with non-stick paper. Make meringue mushrooms. Whisk the egg white until stiff, add 25 g (1 oz) of the sugar and whisk again until stiff. Fold in another 25 g (1 oz) sugar.

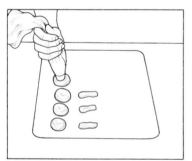

2 Spoon the meringue into a piping bag fitted with a plain nozzle. Pipe the meringue on to the prepared baking sheet to resemble small mushroom caps and stalks. Bake in the oven at 110°C (225°F) mark ¼ for about 1½ hours until dry. Leave to cool for at least 15 minutes.

3 Grease a 33 × 23 cm (13 × 9 inch) Swiss roll tin. Line with greaseproof paper and grease the paper. Dredge with the extra caster sugar then flour, knocking out any excess.

4 Put the eggs and measured caster sugar in a deep bowl which fits snugly inside the rim of a saucepan of simmering water.

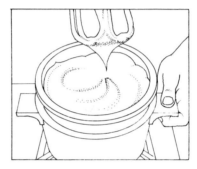

5 Whisk the eggs and sugar until thick enough to leave a trail on the surface when the beaters are lifted. Do not overheat the bowl by letting it come into contact with the simmering water or by having the heat under the saucepan too high.

6 Take the bowl off the saucepan and whisk the mixture for 5 minutes until cool. Sift in the measured flour and cocoa and gently fold through the mixture. Fold in 15 ml (1 tbsp) water.

7 Pour the mixture gently into the prepared tin and lightly level off the surface. Bake in the oven at 200°C (400°F) mark 6 for about 12 minutes until slightly shrunk away from the tin.

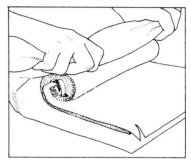

8 Meanwhile, place a sheet of greaseproof paper over a tea towel. Dredge the paper with caster sugar and turn the cake out on to it. Trim off the crusty edges with a sharp knife. Roll up with the paper inside. Transfer to a wire rack, seam side down. Leave to cool for 20 minutes.

9 Put the butter in a bowl and beat until soft. Put the chocolate and 15 ml (1 tbsp) water in a bowl over a pan of hot water. Melt, then leave to cool slightly. Gradually sift and beat the icing sugar into the softened butter, then add the cool chocolate.

10 Unroll the cold Swiss roll and spread the chestnut purée over the surface. Roll up again without the paper inside. Place on a cake board or plate.

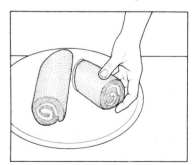

11 Cut a thick diagonal slice off one end of the Swiss roll and attach with butter cream to the side of the roll.

12 Using a piping bag and a large star nozzle, pipe thin lines of butter cream over the log. Pipe 1 or 2 swirls of butter cream to represent knots in the wood. Sandwich the meringues together with a little butter cream to form mushrooms. Decorate the log with the mushrooms and sprigs of holly. Dust lightly with sifted icing sugar. Store in an airtight container for up to 2–3 days.

Menu Suggestion
In France, Bûche de Noël is served on Christmas Eve as a dessert, after the traditional main course of Roast Turkey with Chestnut Stuffing (page 34).

BÛCHE DE NOËL
Bûche de Noël is the traditional cake eaten in France at Christmas time. The tradition of serving this and the English Yule log dates back to the days when a huge log used to be burnt on Christmas Eve.

GINGERBREAD SNOWMEN

1.00* 🖻 £ 303 cals

* plus 30 minutes cooling and 2 hours drying

Makes about 16

350 g (12 oz) plain flour

5 ml (1 tsp) bicarbonate of soda

10 ml (2 tsp) ground ginger

100 g (4 oz) butter or margarine

175 g (6 oz) soft brown sugar

60 ml (4 tbsp) golden syrup

1 egg, beaten

450 g (1 lb) icing sugar

currants, a little marzipan, red food colouring and red ribbon, to decorate

1 Grease 3 baking sheets. Sift the flour, soda and ginger into a bowl. Rub in the butter until the mixture resembles fine breadcrumbs. Add the sugar. Beat the syrup into the egg and stir into the flour mixture. Mix to a dough.

2 Knead the dough until smooth. Divide the dough into 2 and roll out onto a floured surface to 0.5 cm ($\frac{1}{4}$ inch) thickness.

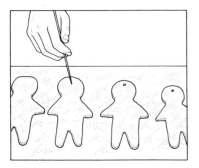

3 Using a cutter, cut out gingerbread men until all the dough has been used. With a skewer, make a small hole at the top of each head. Place on the prepared baking sheets.

4 Bake in the oven at 190°C (375°F) mark 5 for 12–15 minutes until golden brown. Cool slightly, then transfer carefully to a wire rack and leave to cool completely.

5 Sift the icing sugar into a bowl. With a wooden spoon, gradually work in 90 ml (6 tbsp) warm water until the icing is thick enough to coat the back of the spoon. If necessary, add more water or sugar to adjust the consistency.

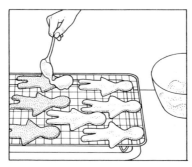

6 Use the icing at once to coat the gingerbread men completely. Place the cooling rack over a baking sheet and coat the icing over the snowmen with a large spoon. While still wet, decorate each one with 2 currants for eyes, 1 for a mouth and 3 currants for buttons. Leave to dry.

7 When completely dry, colour a little marzipan with food colouring. Roll out and cut thin strips to make scarves. Decorate each snowman with a marzipan scarf. Store in an airtight tin.

8 If a piece of ribbon is threaded through the hole, the biscuits can be hung on the Christmas tree for 2–3 days before they are eaten. If wrapped in silver foil, they will last a few days longer and still look pretty on the tree.

FINNISH STAR BISCUITS

| 0.30* | £ | ❄ | 70 cals |

* plus 1 hour chilling and cooling

Makes about 30

75 g (3 oz) black treacle

100 g (4 oz) butter

4 green cardamoms

50 g (2 oz) caster sugar

15 ml (1 tbsp) ground almonds

200 g (7 oz) plain flour

2.5 ml ($\frac{1}{2}$ tsp) bicarbonate of soda

2.5 ml ($\frac{1}{2}$ tsp) ground cinnamon

2.5 ml ($\frac{1}{2}$ tsp) ground ginger

1 egg yolk

coloured ribbon, to decorate

1 Put the treacle and butter in a saucepan and heat gently, stirring occasionally, until melted and blended. Cool slightly for 5 minutes.

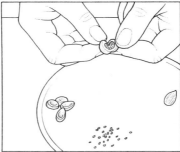

2 Split the cardamom pods open and remove the seeds; crush in a pestle and mortar or in a bowl with the end of a rolling pin.

3 Put all the dry ingredients in a bowl. Make a well in the centre, add the treacle mixture and egg yolk and mix well to form a smooth dough. Wrap in cling film and chill in the refrigerator for at least 30 minutes.

4 Knead the dough on a lightly floured surface, then roll out to just 1 cm ($\frac{1}{2}$ inch) thickness.

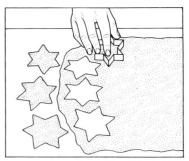

5 Using a 6.5 cm (2$\frac{1}{2}$ inch) star cutter, stamp out about 30 biscuits, re-rolling the dough as necessary.

6 Place the biscuits on baking sheets lined with non-stick baking parchment. Bake in the oven at 190°C (375°F) mark 5 for about 8 minutes.

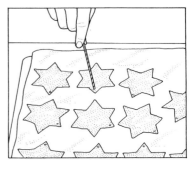

7 Using a skewer, immediately make a small hole near the edge of each star. Transfer to a wire rack and leave to cool for 30 minutes.

8 Thread coloured ribbon through the biscuits to hang on the Christmas tree and to serve. If keeping them for any longer than 8 hours, remove from the tree and pack in an airtight tin.

SPECULAAS
(DUTCH SPICED BISCUITS)

0.45* £ 72 cals

* plus cooling

Makes 18 (see box)

100 g (4 oz) plain white flour
2.5 ml (½ tsp) ground cloves
2.5 ml (½ tsp) ground cinnamon
2.5 ml (½ tsp) ground ginger
pinch of grated nutmeg
pinch of baking powder
pinch of salt
50 g (2 oz) dark soft brown sugar
15 ml (1 tbsp) milk
65 g (2½ oz) butter or margarine
30 ml (2 tbsp) very finely chopped
    candied peel
flaked blanched almonds,
    to decorate

1 Sift the flour, spices, baking powder and salt into a bowl. Put the sugar and milk in a small saucepan and heat gently, stirring, until the sugar has dissolved.

2 Stir the sugar mixture into the bowl. Add the butter in pieces and the candied peel and work to a smooth dough.

3 Turn the dough onto a floured surface and knead lightly until no longer sticky. Roll out the dough to a thickness of 0.5 cm (¼ inch).

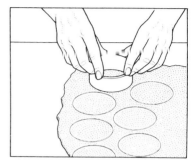

4 Cut the dough into 18 shapes using a 6.5 cm (2½ inch) biscuit cutter (see box) and place on greased baking sheets. Press a few almond pieces into each biscuit, then bake in the oven at 180°C (350°F) mark 4 for 15 minutes.

5 Leave to settle on the sheets for a few minutes, then transfer to a wire rack and leave to cool completely. Store in an airtight tin for up to 2 weeks.

SPECULAAS

The Dutch word *speculaas* comes from the Latin word for mirror—*speculum*. Traditional *speculaas* dough is pressed into special carved wooden moulds and then turned out onto baking sheets, giving a mirror image. At Christmas time in Holland, baker's shops and pâtisseries are full of intricately 'carved' *speculaas*, some as heavy as 450 g (1 lb), and special moulds (mostly in the shape of men and women) are available for home baking. If you are making them at home without a special mould, you can use gingerbread men cutters, in which case you will be able to make about 6 men.

MELOMACAROUNA
(CYPRIOT ALMOND AND HONEY COOKIES)

| 1.30 | 🍴 🍴 £ £ | 214 cals |

Makes about 30

125 ml (4 fl oz) vegetable oil
125 ml (4 fl oz) evaporated milk
100 g (4 oz) butter, softened
finely grated rind of 1 orange
50 ml (2 fl oz) orange juice
7.5 ml ($\frac{1}{2}$ tbsp) lemon juice
225 g (8 oz) granulated sugar
pinch of salt
165 g ($5\frac{1}{2}$ oz) fine semolina
375 g (13 oz) plain flour
7.5 ml ($\frac{1}{2}$ tbsp) bicarbonate of soda
125 g (4 oz) ground almonds
2.5 ml ($\frac{1}{2}$ tsp) ground cinnamon
90 ml (6 tbsp) clear honey

1 Put the oil in a bowl with the evaporated milk, butter, orange rind and juice, lemon juice, half of the sugar and the salt. Beat well.

2 Gradually add the semolina and the flour sifted with the bicarbonate of soda, and mix to a stiff dough. Turn onto a floured work surface and knead well.

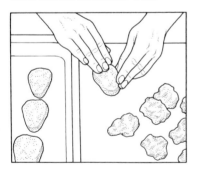

3 With your hands, form small pieces of the mixture into 30 almond shapes, about 7.5 cm (3 inches) long and 4 cm ($1\frac{1}{2}$ inches) wide. Place on greased baking sheets. spacing them well apart. Bake in 2 batches in the oven at 180°C (350°F) mark 4 for 30 minutes. Transfer to a wire rack and leave to cool slightly.

4 Meanwhile, mix the ground almonds and cinnamon together on a large flat plate. Set aside. Put the remaining sugar in a heavy-based, small saucepan, with the honey and 125 ml (4 fl oz) water. Heat gently until the sugar has dissolved, then simmer for 3–4 minutes. Remove the froth from the surface of the liquid with a slotted spoon.

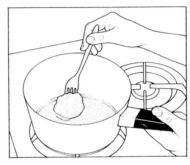

5 Turn the heat down to very low and dip the melo-macarouna in the syrup one at a time, turning gently with a fork to ensure even coating.

6 Lift out of the syrup with the fork, transfer to the plate of almonds and cinnamon and coat thoroughly, using your fingertips to pat the mixture on. Return to the wire rack and leave to dry and cool. Store in an airtight tin for up to 2 weeks.

MELOMACAROUNA

Melomacarouna are traditionally eaten in Cyprus during the Christmas period. Their name comes from the Greek words 'melo' meaning honey, and 'macarouna' meaning almond, the two main flavours of these delicious sweetmeats. For speed and ease, make them with an electric mixer.

FRUIT SALAMI

| 0.45* | 🖯 | £ £ | 263–307 cals |

* plus overnight chilling
Makes 12–14 slices

100 g (4 oz) blanched almonds

225 g (8 oz) mixed dried whole fruit (eg apricots, figs, dates), unsoaked

100 g (4 oz) dark chocolate

50 g (2 oz) glacé cherries, chopped

100 g (4 oz) dark soft brown sugar

175 g (6 oz) unsalted butter

1 egg, beaten

cocoa powder, for dredging

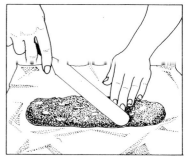

1 Chop the nuts and dried fruit finely. Discard any stones from the fruit.

2 Break the chocolate in pieces into a heatproof bowl standing over a saucepan of gently simmering water. Add the rum and heat gently until chocolate has melted, stirring only once or twice after the chocolate has started to melt.

3 Add the sugar and butter and stir over gentle heat until the sugar has dissolved, then remove from the heat and beat in the chopped fruit and nuts and the egg. Continue beating until mixture cools.

4 Place the mixture on a sheet of non-stick baking parchment and form into two sausage shapes, about 5 cm (2 inches) thick. Wrap in the paper and chill in the refrigerator overnight.

5 To serve, unwrap and dredge liberally with icing sugar. Cut into diagonal slices while still chilled, then arrange on a serving plate. Allow to come to room temperature for about 30 minutes before serving.

FRUIT SALAMI

This after-dinner sweetmeat is similar to a Christmas speciality from Czechoslovakia, where it is called *ovocný salám*. There are many different versions, some made with all dried fruit and no chocolate, and some with honey rather than butter. This version is very fruity, and is best made with the kind of dried fruits which are sold at health food shops. These fruits are plump, juicy and full of flavour, because they have been dried naturally in the sun. Choose whichever fruits you like best, bearing in mind that the salami will look most attractive when sliced if the fruits contrast well in colour, as they do in the photograph.

Food for Presents

There is nothing nicer than giving—or receiving—a present that is home-made. Edible presents are especially welcome, because they show that time and trouble has been spent, and they generally taste fresher than their commercial counterparts. Presentation is all-important with edible presents, so turn to pages 146–149 for ideas on packaging.

SHORTBREAD

| 1.05 | ⬠ | £ | ✳ | 1770 cals |

Serves 6–8

150 g (5 oz) plain flour

45 ml (3 tbsp) rice flour

50 g (2 oz) caster sugar

100 g (4 oz) butter

caster sugar, for dredging

1 Sift the flours into a bowl and add the sugar. Work in the butter with your fingertips — keep it in one piece and gradually work in the dry ingredients. Knead well.

2 Pack into a floured shortbread mould, then turn out on to a baking sheet. Alternatively, pack into an 18 cm (7 inch) sandwich tin, prick well with a fork and pinch up the edges decoratively with finger and thumb.

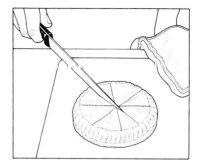

3 Bake in the oven at 170°C (325°F) mark 3 for about 45 minutes, until firm and pale golden. Mark into 6–8 triangles while still hot. If using a sandwich tin, cool slightly before turning out on to a wire rack.

4 When cool, dredge with sugar. Serve cut into wedges. Store in an airtight tin. To give as a Christmas present, tie with a piece of red ribbon. Wrap in cling film or foil or pack in a box.

SHORTBREAD

Shortbread is made all year round, but it has a particular significance in Scotland at Hogmanay, when it is served to 'first footers' who arrive after midnight on New Year's Eve. First footers are thought to bring luck, so it is the Scottish custom to make them as welcome as possible, and to offer them food and drink — usually shortbread, Black Bun (page 101) and tots of whisky.

Traditional Scottish shortbread moulds are made with a thistle design in the centre. These can be bought at specialist kitchen shops, but they are not essential; an ordinary sandwich cake tin will do the job just as well.

Be sure to use a good-quality butter when making shortbread. The flavour of shortbread relies heavily on the butter in the mixture, and margarine makes a poor substitute.

MARZIPAN PETITS FOURS

| 0.30 | £ | 70 cals |

Makes about 35

450 g (1 lb) good-quality marzipan
or almond paste (see box)

10 blanched almonds or walnut
halves

20 large glacé cherries

45 ml (3 tbsp) chopped walnuts

45 ml (3 tbsp) pistachio nuts

1 Divide the marzipan into 3
equal portions. Knead until
smooth.

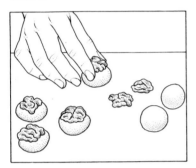

2 Roll 1 portion into 10 balls,
flatten slightly, then press an
almond or walnut half on top of
each one. Set aside.

3 Divide the remaining
marzipan into 20. Roll each
piece into a ball, flatten slightly
and roll around each cherry. Roll
half in the chopped walnuts and
half in the pistachio nuts to coat.
Cut each ball into quarters.

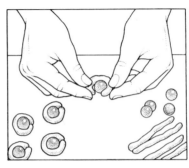

4 Alternatively, roll the
marzipan into thin strips and
use to surround the glacé cherries
so that the cherries show top and
bottom. Roll in the nuts as in step
3. Cut in half.

5 Arrange the petits fours in
sweet cases in a decorative
box, alternating the different
designs in rows to make an
attractive display. Store, covered,
in a cool place for up to 1 week.

MARZIPAN PETITS FOURS
Most supermarkets and
delicatessens sell two types of
marzipan or almond paste. For
these petits fours, choose the
white rather than the yellow
variety; it has a better texture
and flavour, and will not affect
the food colouring quite so
much. White-coloured marzipan
is almost like home-made, which
can also be used. See the recipe
for Almond Paste on page 140.

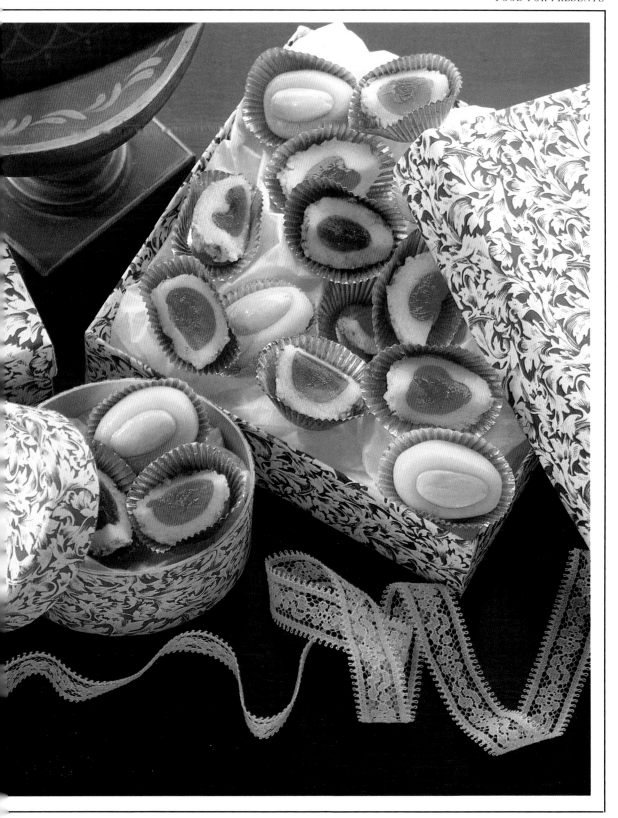

RICH CHOCOLATE RUM TRUFFLES

0.45*	🎩	£	✳	69 cals

* plus 24 minutes cooling and 2–2½
hours setting

Makes 24

225 g (8 oz) plain chocolate

25 g (1 oz) butter

2 egg yolks

10 ml (2 tsp) dark rum

10 ml (2 tsp) single cream

drinking chocolate powder or
    chocolate vermicelli, to decorate

1 Break the chocolate in pieces
into a heatproof bowl standing
over a saucepan of gently simmering water. Heat gently until the
chocolate has melted, stirring only
once or twice after the chocolate
has started to melt. Leave to cool
for about 4 minutes.

2 Beat in the butter, egg yolks,
rum and cream and stir until
the mixture is thick enough to
handle. Leave to cool for about 20
minutes, then chill for 1–1½ hours
until firm enough to handle.

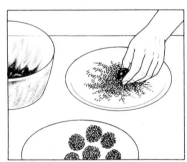

3 Form the mixture into small
balls and roll in chocolate
powder or vermicelli. Leave for 1
hour until firm.

4 Arrange the truffles in sweet
cases in a decorative box. Store
in the refrigerator for up to 1 week.

COLLETTES

1.40* 🍫 🍫 £ 93 cals

* plus 2 hours setting

Makes 16

190 g (6½ oz) plain chocolate
25 g (1 oz) butter
10 ml (2 tsp) brandy
60 ml (4 tbsp) double cream
flaked almonds, glacé cherries and
crystallised violets, to decorate

1 Arrange 16 small paper cases on a baking sheet.

2 Break 100 g (4 oz) of the chocolate in pieces into a heat-proof bowl standing over a sauce-pan of gently simmering water. Heat gently until the chocolate has melted, stirring only once or twice after the chocolate has started to melt. Remove bowl from pan.

3 Spoon a little chocolate into each case and, using a clean paint brush, coat the inside of each paper case. Leave to set in a cool place for about 1 hour.

4 Coat again making sure the chocolate forms an even layer. Leave to set in a cool place for about 1 hour, then carefully peel away the paper from the cases.

5 Melt the remaining chocolate with the butter as in step 2, leave for about 5 minutes until cool but not set, then stir in the brandy until evenly mixed.

6 Whip the cream until stiff and fold into the chocolate mixture. Leave to set for about 5 minutes, until the mixture is thick enough for piping.

7 Spoon the chocolate cream into a piping bag fitted with a small star nozzle and pipe into the chocolate cases. Decorate with a flaked almond, a piece of cherry or a crystallised violet.

8 Arrange the collettes in clean paper cases in a decorative box. Store in the refrigerator. They will keep fresh for up to 1 week.

COLLETTES

Collettes are chocolate petits fours. In France, they are often decorated with gold leaf or pistachio nuts rather than the decoration used here. Petits fours are so called because they were originally baked in small ovens. In the 17th century, the famous chef La Varenne recom-mended that pâtissiers used small ovens for baking small quantities.

RUMTOPF

£ £

see box below

450 g (1 lb) prepared fruit (see box)
225 g (8 oz) caster sugar to every 450 g (1 lb) prepared fruit
rum, brandy or kirsch

1 Take a large, deep, glazed stone or pottery jar with a wide neck and tightly fitting lid (not metal) and a saucer that will fit inside it; clean *thoroughly*.

2 Carefully wash the fruit and dry on absorbent kitchen paper. Berry fruits should be hulled; currants, gooseberries and grapes stalked. Skin large-stoned fruits if you like, then halve them and remove the stones.

3 Remove the tough flesh and outer skin of fruits like pineapples; dip banana slices in lemon juice; peel, core and slice pears; scrub the skin of oranges and slice into rings.

4 Spread the first fruit on a plate; sprinkle with the sugar and turn gently so that every part of the fruit is covered. Leave for about 1 hour.

5 Transfer the fruit and sugar to the jar and spread evenly. Completely cover with alcohol.

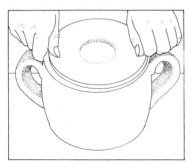

6 Place the saucer on top to keep the fruit submerged, then cover the jar tightly with cling film and cover with the lid. Store in a cool, dry place.

7 Repeat the process, replacing a clean saucer each time and resealing the jar as before. Stir the contents or, alternatively, leave in the original layers.

8 When the last batch of fruit has been added, top up with more alcohol, cover and label. Store for at least 1 month. Check the level of the liquid occasionally and add more if necessary.

RUMTOPF

This is a delicious way of preserving fresh fruit with sugar and alcohol, by layering two or more different types over a period of time, as they come into season. Rum is used in the original German recipe, but brandy or a liqueur such as kirsch are equally suitable. Choose ripe, unblemished fruit for best results. Most fruits are suitable, except rhubarb, which tends to give a bitter taste, and apples, which may ferment. Soft fruits such as raspberries, loganberries and currants are delicious, but they will disintegrate with time. Very watery fruits like melons should be kept to a minimum as they dilute the alcohol, which may result in mould growth or fermentation. You can make as much or as little as you like, therefore the number of calories depends on how much is used.

RASPBERRY LIQUEUR CONSERVE

$0.35*$ £ 975 cals

* plus 1 hour 20 minutes standing
and 3 months maturing

Makes two 450 g (1 lb) jars

450 g (1 lb) raspberries

450 g (1 lb) granulated sugar

15 ml (1 tbsp) kirsch or brandy

1 Put the raspberries and sugar in separate ovenproof dishes. Cook in the oven at 180°C (350°F) mark 4 for 15 minutes.

2 Turn the raspberries and sugar into a large bowl and stir for a few minutes. Leave to stand for 20 minutes. Repeat the stirring and standing 3 times.

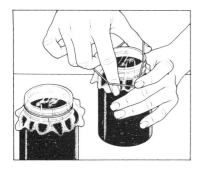

3 Add the kirsch or brandy, then pot in jars. Place a disc of waxed paper across the surface of the conserve, then cover the jar with dampened Cellophane. Secure with an elastic band, label and leave in a cool, dark place for at least 3 months.

RASPBERRY LIQUEUR CONSERVE

This conserve tastes absolutely delicious, because the natural flavour of the fruit is preserved without boiling. It will keep for at least 12 months and can be used just like ordinary jam, but it is especially good with croissants.

ROSEMARY APPLE JELLY

2.00* 🍴🍴 1020 cals

* plus 12 hours straining

Makes about six 450 g (1 lb) jars

2.3 kg (5 lb) cooking apples

30 ml (2 tbsp) fresh rosemary leaves

1.1 litres (2 pints) malt vinegar

granulated or preserving sugar

green food colouring

sprigs of fresh rosemary

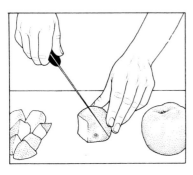

1 Remove any bruised or damaged portions from the apples and chop them roughly into thick chunks without peeling or coring.

2 Put the apples in a preserving pan with 1.1 litres (2 pints) water and the rosemary. Bring to the boil, then simmer for about 45 minutes until soft and pulpy. Stir from time to time to prevent sticking. Add the vinegar and boil for a further 5 minutes.

3 Spoon the apple pulp into a jelly bag or cloth attached to the legs of an upturned stool. Allow the juice to strain into a large bowl for at least 12 hours. Do not squeeze the bag or the jelly will be cloudy. Discard the pulp.

4 Measure the extract and return to the pan with 450 g (1 lb) sugar to every 600 ml (1 pint) extract. Stir until the sugar has dissolved.

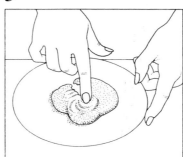

5 Bring to the boil and boil rapidly, without stirring, for about 10 minutes until setting point is reached, when a temperature of 105°C (221°F) is reached on a sugar thermometer. (If you do not have a sugar thermometer, test that the jelly has reached setting point by spooning a little on to a chilled saucer. Leave it to cool, then push a finger across the surface. When setting point has been reached, the surface will wrinkle.)

6 Remove the pan from the heat. Skim the surface with a slotted spoon to remove any scum. Add a few drops of colouring and stir.

7 Pour into warmed jars and add a sprig of rosemary to each. Place a disc of waxed paper across the surface of the jelly, then cover the jar with dampened Cellophane. Secure with an elastic band and label. Store in a cool, dry, dark place for up to 1 year.

ROSEMARY APPLE JELLY

The rosemary flavouring in this jelly goes particularly well with roast lamb or grilled lamb chops. For a different flavour, substitute a few rose geranium leaves or lemon balm leaves for the rosemary. For a delicate rose-coloured jelly, add a few red berries to the apples.

SPICED APRICOT AND RAISIN CHUTNEY

1.25* £ 1584 cals

* plus 2–3 months maturing

Makes about 1.4 kg (3 lb)

225 g (8 oz) dried apricots, soaked overnight

350 g (12 oz) onions, skinned

finely grated rind and juice of 1 orange

1 garlic clove, skinned and crushed

50 g (2 oz) seedless raisins

225 g (8 oz) granulated sugar

5 ml (1 tsp) prepared mustard

1.25 ml ($\frac{1}{4}$ tsp) ground cinnamon

1.25 ml ($\frac{1}{4}$ tsp) ground mixed spice

5 ml (1 tsp) salt

450 ml ($\frac{3}{4}$ pint) malt vinegar

1 Drain the apricots and chop roughly. Discard the water. Chop the onions finely.

2 Place the prepared ingredients in a medium saucepan with the orange rind and juice. Add all the remaining ingredients and bring slowly to the boil.

3 Boil gently, uncovered, stirring occasionally for about 1 hour, or until the chutney is thick, well reduced and no excess liquid remains.

4 Pour into warmed jars, cover with airtight, vinegar-proof tops and label. Store in a cool, dry dark place for 2–3 months to mature before eating.

VANILLA FUDGE

| 0.50* | 🍴 🍴 ❋ | 77 cals |

* plus 2–3 hours cooling

Makes about 36 pieces

450 g (1 lb) granulated sugar
75 g (3 oz) unsalted butter
150 ml (¼ pint) milk
170 g (6 oz) can evaporated milk
2.5 ml (½ tsp) vanilla flavouring

1 Brush a shallow 18 cm (7 inch) square cake tin lightly with oil.

2 Put the sugar, butter and milk in a heavy-based saucepan. Heat slowly, stirring all the time, until the sugar dissolves and the butter melts.

3 Bring to the boil and continue boiling for 10–15 minutes until a temperature of 116°C (240°F) or soft ball stage is reached on a sugar thermometer. (Or when a little mixture dropped into a cup of cold water forms a soft ball when rolled between finger and thumb.) It is important that the mixture is stirred constantly while boiling to prevent it sticking and burning.

4 Remove the pan from the heat, add the vanilla flavouring and beat the mixture with a wooden spoon until it feels thick and grainy and begins to lose its gloss. Pour the mixture into the prepared tin and leave for about 5–10 minutes until almost set.

5 Mark the soft fudge into squares, then leave for 2–3 hours to cool completely before cutting and removing from the tin. Store between sheets of waxed paper in an airtight container for up to 2–3 weeks.

——————— VARIATION ———————

Peanut Butter Fudge
Follow the recipe for Vanilla Fudge but use only 50 g (2 oz) unsalted butter with 150 g (5 oz) crunchy peanut butter and replace the evaporated milk with 30 ml (2 tbsp) golden syrup.

ORANGE SLICES IN COINTREAU

1.15* £ £ 970 cals

* plus 30 minutes cooling and 1 month maturing

Makes about two 450 g (1 lb) jars

350 g (12 oz) granulated sugar

6 firm oranges

1 small cinnamon stick

5 ml (1 tsp) cloves

150 ml ($\frac{1}{4}$ pint) Cointreau

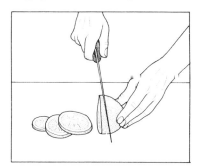

1 Put the sugar and 450 ml ($\frac{3}{4}$ pint) water in a saucepan. Heat gently until the sugar has dissolved, then bring to the boil. Boil for 1 minute, then add a further 450 ml ($\frac{3}{4}$ pint) water.

2 Scrub the orange skins clean. Cut the oranges into 0.5 cm ($\frac{1}{4}$ inch) thick slices.

3 Add the oranges and spices to the sugar syrup and poach gently for about 45 minutes until tender. Remove from the heat and drain, reserving the syrup but removing the cinnamon stick. Leave to cool for about 30 minutes.

4 Arrange the fruit in jars, adding a few of the cloves. Add the liqueur to the remaining syrup and pour over the orange slices. Cover at once with airtight tops, label and leave to mature for at least 1 month.

BRANDIED PEACHES

1.00* ⬚ ⬚ £ £ 570 cals

* plus 1 hour cooling and 3 months maturing

Makes about three 450 g (1 lb) jars

900 g (2 lb) fresh peaches

250 g (8 oz) granulated sugar

about 225 ml (8 fl oz) brandy

1 Skin the peaches. Plunge them into boiling water, then gently peel off the skins with your fingers. Halve the peaches and remove the stones.

2 Put 125 g (4 oz) of the sugar and 300 ml ($\frac{1}{2}$ pint) water in a saucepan and heat gently until the sugar has dissolved. Add the peaches to the syrup and poach gently for 4–5 minutes. Drain, reserving the syrup, and leave to cool for about 30 minutes.

3 Arrange the fruit in jars. Add the remaining sugar to the reserved syrup and dissolve it slowly. Bring to the boil and boil to 110°C (230°F) on a sugar thermometer. Allow to cool for about 30 minutes.

4 Measure the syrup and add an equal quantity of brandy. Pour over the peaches. Cover at once with airtight tops, label and leave for at least 3 months.

——— VARIATION ———

Brandied Cherries
Use 450 g (1 lb) fresh cherries to replace the peaches. Prick the cherries all over with a darning needle, then poach in the syrup and continue as in the recipe above.

APRICOT LIQUEUR

0.35* £ £ 2964 cals

*plus 5–6 days standing and 1 month maturing

Makes about 1.5 litres (2$\frac{1}{2}$ pints)

450 g (1 lb) apricots, washed

450 g (1 lb) granulated sugar

70 cl bottle of dry white wine

300 ml ($\frac{1}{2}$ pint) gin

1 Cut the apricots in half and remove the stones. Crack the stones and remove the kernels from inside, then blanch the kernels in boiling water for 1 minute.

2 Place the apricots, sugar and wine in a saucepan and heat gently, stirring, until the sugar has dissolved. Bring to the boil, then remove from the heat.

3 Stir in the gin and apricot kernels. Pour into a large bowl or jug, cover tightly and leave for 5–6 days.

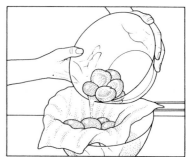

4 Strain through muslin, then bottle the liqueur and label. Leave in a cool, dark place for at least 1 month before using.

USEFUL INFORMATION
AND
BASIC RECIPES

Christmas Around the World

Wherever there are Christians, Christmas is celebrated with feasting and family gatherings. The actual date of the festival varies: the Western church celebrates on 25th December, the Eastern Orthodox on 6th January. For some the religious festival is separated from the feasting and present-giving, but one way or another, between early December and early January there are Christians somewhere celebrating their great day.

In many countries, St. Nicholas, in the form of Sinter Klaas, Sant Nikolaus, Santa Claus and other

Children's favourite Christmas symbol around the world

The first givers of Christmas gifts

variations, has become a part of Christmas. He is the patron saint of children. The original Nicholas was a bishop in that part of the eastern Mediterranean that is now Turkey. Stories tell of his remarkable childhood; he was selected to high office in the church while still little more than a boy. And it is for his special love for children that he is remembered.

The festival of St. Nicholas is on 6th December. It is, therefore, natural that the celebration of this saint's day has somewhat merged with the one that marks Christ's birth, so soon afterwards.

The Dutch are probably the first to set the ball rolling with their Sinter Klaas festivities. The main day for feasting, merry-making and present giving in the Netherlands is 6th December. This is the children's day and a public holiday.

Christmas itself is altogether quieter, celebrated in a primarily religious way. Throughout the season there are chestnuts and *speculaas* (page 113), doughnuts and apple fritters, Christmas shortbread and fancy fondants. Fancy cakes and pastries in the form of initials *(letterhanketten)* are also popular.

Much of central Europe celebrates in the same way, starting with St. Nicholas, and going on until the Epiphany on 6th January. Epiphany is yet another excuse for gift giving. This is the feast of the Three Kings who brought gifts of gold, frankincense and myrrh. In between the religious ceremonies, feasting centres around pork, either fresh or cured, and seasonal pickles and preserves. *Stollen* (page 99), a rich, yeast cake is made at this time of year in Germany.

Unusual German tree decorations

Lebkuchen, (spiced biscuits) and gingerbreads abound. These are often hung on the tree.

In France, gift giving starts on St. Nicholas. But the main Christmas feast, the *réveillon*, is held after Midnight Mass on Christmas Eve. The centre of the meal is roast turkey or goose, and there will be baked ham, game and rich and expensive delicacies like truffles and foie gras.

As in most countries, the cake is important, it is traditionally shaped like a log, the *Bûche de Noël* (page 108). Sometimes decorated with chocolate, but more traditionally with a chestnut-flavoured cream—this is the height of the chestnut season.

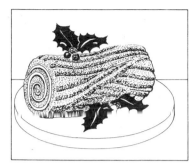

A traditional Bûche de Noël

The Italians keep their main gift giving for the end of the Christmas season, at Epiphany. But celebrations start eight days before Christmas, with children, sometimes adults, going from house to house reciting and singing Christmas songs. The children are rewarded with money to buy the traditional seasonal sweets and biscuits.

The day before Christmas Eve is a fast, but the family meal that follows makes up for that, with all the richest food that can be mustered. Rich meats and cakes abound, with seasonal vegetables and summer fruits preserved in the local brandy (page 144), to do justice to the occasion.

Further north, in the British Isles, the build-up to Christmas starts in Advent; but all the gift giving and celebrations centre around Christmas and the New Year. Epiphany is almost completely secularised into Twelfth Night, or the official end to the holiday season.

Religious observances start with carol singing, which may be in aid of charity or simply as an act of worship. The birth of Christ is then first celebrated at midnight on Christmas Eve, and after that Santa can come.

Few lay people in Great Britain would know of the ancient connection between Santa Claus and that boy bishop from Turkey; most people see the gift giving as a way of celebrating the birthday of Christ. But the family is central to all the celebrations. Entertainments are largely geared to the children and the festive meal is a family one.

Nowadays, turkey is the most usual meat on the Christmas menu in Great Britain, though not so long ago goose, duck or game would have been served. Pork is also a Christmas meat, though more commonly served in the form of ham. With the turkey are served traditional winter vegetables. A rich plum pudding,

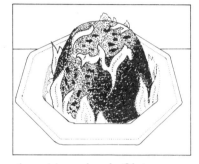

An exciting end to the Christmas dinner—a flaming pudding!

flaming in brandy, follows the turkey, and mince pies are always available for guests who drop in for drinks or coffee. The Christmas cake is a rich, dark fruit cake, coated in almond paste and iced with royal icing.

The Irish celebrate less lavishly and a large joint of beef is more popular than the English turkey. The Scots, too, keep their Christmas more simply than the English, saving their big reunions for New Year's Eve. Gifts are exchanged at Christmas, but it is at Hogmanay (New Year's Eve) that the black bun and shortbread come out, drink flows freely and family, friends and strangers are all gathered into the festivities.

Travelling still further north, we reach Scandinavia. Here the cooking traditions of several nations begin to merge. There are distinctions between the Christmas celebrations in Denmark, Finland, Sweden and Norway, but they are blurred by many similarities.

Many of the shared features are the result of climate. This is the dark time of year in these northern countries, when daylight is shorter than anywhere else in the world. So candles appear everywhere. Candles are used to decorate the tree, and tables and living rooms are lit by candlelight.

Celebrations start here, not with St. Nicholas but with St. Lucia. Her day is 13th December, and is celebrated first with candles, then with buns, cakes and spiced biscuits. The baking goes on to contribute a major part to the Christmas feasting. Gingerbread, spiced cakes and sweet, yeasty doughs abound throughout the season. In many homes a show loaf is made—just flour and water, very decorative and heavily glazed. This is not for eating but for ornament and will end up being fed to the birds.

The biggest family meal of a Scandinavian Christmas is on Christmas Eve. In most homes the main dish will be pork, probably a roast loin, crisp with crackling (page 42). The *julskinka* (page 47), or Christmas ham also invariably appears. In Norway, Finland and Sweden there will also be *lutfisk*, which is a dried and cured fish. Other popular Christmas meats are goose, duck, chicken and various sausages. The meal will most likely end with *risengrød* (page 44), a sweet rice pudding, served with a tart cherry sauce.

On Christmas Day and for several days afterwards there will be a great *smörgåsbord*, and all guests will be expected to eat something—to refuse is considered impolite.

Wooden Swedish candle-holder

Special Ingredients

Many of the traditional festive foods of Christmas are luxuries that we don't buy the rest of the year. With such unfamiliar foods it is often difficult to know what to look for when buying them, let alone how to cook or store them. Storage is often a problem because the sheer quantity of food puts extra pressure on refrigerator space.

You need to consider storage even before you buy your Christmas foods. If you are going to bring home large items like a whole Stilton or a large ham—not to mention the turkey—there is no way they will fit into a normal domestic refrigerator along with its usual load of everyday foods. So where else can they go?

In Europe, the December weather may be your friend here. The average refrigerator maintains a temperature between 2° and 7°C (35° and 45°F); all you need to supplement it is somewhere else that maintains that temperature. So long as the weather is not unseasonably mild, the answer is outside. Any outside storeroom, the garden shed or garage, even the back porch, will all be pretty cold—check the temperature with a thermometer if you are at all worried. But you do need to be sure that your food storage is clean and protected from animals and insects; make full use of modern storage aids like plastic boxes and trays, foil, cling film, polythene bags and the insulated picnic box you use in summer.

CHEESES

A whole or half Stilton is a favourite Christmas treat. While the cheese is still whole it needs no special treatment; the rind keeps the cheese in good condition if it is stored at about 7°C (45°F).

But once the rind is cut the cheese will start to deteriorate. To prevent it drying, cover the cut surfaces with a cloth wrung out in a salt and water solution. This way it should remain in good condition for about 2 weeks.

Smaller pieces can be wrapped in cling film or foil and kept in the refrigerator for about a month. Stilton also freezes quite well, but pack it in small portions because it deteriorates quickly once thawed and you will want to be able to eat it up within a day or two.

To serve the Stilton, don't dig into the centre with a spoon and leave the outside to spoil and

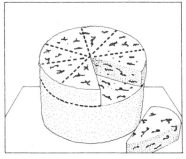

Dividing Stilton into wedges

harden. Cut a full slice across the top and divide it into wedges. Before serving, bring the cut piece to room temperature, loosening any wrapping first so that the cheese doesn't sweat.

HAM AND GAMMON

A ham is the leg of a pig cut from the carcass and cured and matured separately. There are several well-known cures, such as York, Bradenham, Suffolk and others. Most hams are sold ready cooked.

If you want to cook it yourself you will probably (though not invariably) have to buy gammon. Gammon is a bacon cut, cured with the whole side of the pig and cut after curing. The methods of curing are slightly different from those used for ham, so boiled or baked gammon does not taste exactly the same as cooked ham, but it is still an excellent Christmas joint.

Some hams are very salty and need soaking thoroughly before cooking. Ask your butcher's advice about soaking times.

A fresh gammon or ham joint will keep for up to 10 days before cooking if you wrap it tightly in foil to exclude the air and keep it at 2°–7°C (35°–45°F). A vacuum-packed joint will keep for up to 3 weeks at that temperature.

After cooking, wrap it tightly again and store at the same temperature; it should be safe for about a week. Try to keep it in the piece, slicing only as much as you need at any one time, as cut surfaces dry out more quickly.

Bacon and ham do not freeze well, but should be alright if frozen for up to 3 weeks.

To boil a joint weighing 4.5 kg (10 lb) or more your first problem will be a large enough pan. A preserving pan covered tightly with foil is usually the answer. Start timing the cooking after the water reaches boiling point, allowing 15 minutes per 450 g (1 lb) and 15 minutes over. If you started with a joint taken straight from cold storage you may need a little longer. When the meat is cooked, the internal temperature should register a minimum of 70°C (160°F) on a meat thermometer.

To bake the joint, wrap it in foil, place it in a roasting tin and bake at 180°C (350°F) mark 4 for 15 minutes per 450 g (1 lb), with no time over. To glaze it, strip off

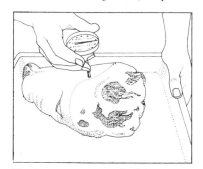

Testing temperature of a joint

the skin (this is also a good test that the meat is cooked—if the skin doesn't come off easily it is not cooked). Spread the glaze over the surface and bake uncovered for another 15 minutes at 200°C (400°F) mark 6.

SMOKED SALMON

Wrap smoked salmon tightly in cling film or foil and store in the refrigerator for no more than a week; the same time limit applies to vacuum-packed salmon. It is not a good idea to freeze smoked salmon at home as it loses colour and flavour.

If you buy frozen vacuum-packed smoked salmon that is quite a different matter. Unopened, it will keep in good condition in the freezer for 6 months. Once thawed, treat as for fresh smoked salmon.

CAVIAR

To keep caviar in perfect condition it needs storing at a constant temperature of 0°C (32°F); even slight variations over a long period can spoil the quality. An unopened jar will only keep for 1 week in the refrigerator; after opening, serve it straight from the fridge, really cold. Cover any that

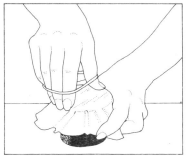

Covering tightly to preserve quality

is left tightly, to exclude as much air as possible, and refrigerate again for up to 3 days. Never freeze caviar.

NUTS

Don't buy your Christmas nuts too early. Although nuts do keep quite well, there is a danger that the earliest nuts that appear may actually be those leftover from last season. Fresh nuts should feel heavy in the shell; older ones dry out and may rattle when shaken.

At home, nuts in the shell will keep for up to 3 months in a cool, dark place. Bring them into the living room only a few at a time. If they are hard to crack, put them in boiling water for 10–12 minutes to soften the shells slightly. To shell chestnuts, slit the shells first with a sharp knife before you soak them in boiling water.

DATES

Dried dates are carefully packaged and keep quite well, but fresh dates are less amenable. In a polythene bag in the refrigerator, they will keep for up to a week, or left out in a cool place they will be alright for 3–4 days. If the skin is

Squeezing dates gently to remove the skin

tough, remove the stalk and squeeze gently between thumb and finger—the fruit will easily slip out of the skin.

OLIVES

Vacuum-packed olives always seem less briny, more like the fresh fruit, than those sold in jars, but storing any left over is not so easy. When you open the pack, transfer the liquid to a plastic container. Then immerse any leftover olives in the liquid, place a slice of lemon on top and seal the lid tightly. Store in the refrigerator. Store opened jars in the same way.

CRANBERRIES

If these hardy berries are in good condition when you buy them, they will keep in the refrigerator for 8 months. They will of course freeze too, for up to 12 months.

Countdown to Christmas

The best Christmas is packed with people and parties, there is lots of food and everybody relaxes. But somebody has to organise it and do the cooking. If that person is you, you could be anything but relaxed by the time the turkey is on the table. To cut the headaches and keep yourself smiling, plan ahead and do as much of the work as you can before the pressure builds up.

HOLIDAY MENU PLANNING

The only meal for which you can lay down a fixed menu far in advance will be the Christmas dinner itself. But it is as well to have some ideas about what you might want to serve on Christmas Eve, as a second meal on Christmas Day, and for any subsequent days when the family are on holiday. Build as much flexibility into these as you can to allow for extra guests, dishes that won't spoil if youngsters opt for going elsewhere—and if they can be meals that will cook themselves while you go out or put your feet up, so much the better.

USING FRESH SEASONAL VEGETABLES

Your freezer will help with holiday meals—but don't fall into the dull trap of living totally on frozen foods. A casserole that you can make ahead and freeze and which will thaw in the oven while you are out on Boxing Day, can be served with a crisp salad based on celery or chicory, both of which are good at Christmastime. Carrots make a seasonal salad too, with nuts, raisins and titbits of fresh fruit.

Leftover turkey, itself served cold, is delicious with hot fresh vegetables. Try braised red cabbage and a purée of Jerusalem artichokes, or slices of aubergine dipped in egg, coated with fresh breadcrumbs and fried until crisp and brown (these can be prepared ahead and frozen if you want). Beetroot always adds colour to the Christmas table, but remember it doesn't have to be in a salad; served hot in a smooth béchamel sauce it tastes slightly sweet and will tempt most palates. Purée of beetroot, served in tiny shortcrust tartlet cases, makes a pretty

Spooning purée into tartlet cases

garnish too. Leeks make a good supper dish: layer them with ham, spoon over a little béchamel sauce, sprinkle with breadcrumbs and grated Parmesan and serve 'au gratin'.

FOREIGN INFLUENCES

You can make use of seasonal home-produced vegetables in new ways to jazz up your Christmas menus. There are usually plenty of cauliflowers around in December, which may be slightly dull if served alone. For a change,

Chopped spring onions enhance flavour

and to make one go further, break it into tiny florets, blanch them lightly, then stir fry with sliced leeks, mushrooms and a flavouring of soy sauce and sherry. If you can find a few spring onions to chop and sprinkle over the top, the flavour will be all the better.

FRESH FRUIT DESSERTS

Light fruit desserts will be welcome as a change from rich

Christmas pudding and mince pies. Oranges are at their best in winter, and have always been traditional Christmas fruits. Slice them and serve in caramel as a simple but seasonal 'pud', or divide into segments and mix with grapefruit segments or the basis of a fruit salad.

A good pineapple needs no dressing up at all. Just peel and

Removing pineapple core

slice it, removing the core, and serve just as it is, with whipped cream. If you think your guests can still manage more alcohol, spoon a little kirsch over it and allow to soak for a few minutes before serving. Treats like fresh dates and tangerines can be handed round with the cheese.

Whether you can serve any of these lovely seasonal fruits and vegetables will depend on careful shopping. Choose only the best and buy no more than about 2 days before Christmas. Then store them carefully—and treat your family and friends to some really thoughtful cooking.

PLANNING AHEAD

October is none too early to be thinking about Christmas, difficult though it may seem. If you do a little autumnal cooking, the spread you can offer over the holiday season will be all the more interesting. Autumn is the perfect time for chutneys and relishes— catch the last of your outdoor tomatoes that refuse to ripen and make green tomato chutney; use windfalls for apple chutney. While plums are still in season, steep some in brandy (page 41)—they make cold roast pork and baked ham taste marvellous. And use the tiny button onions for pickling.

Make your Christmas puddings in late October or early November too. When they are cooked, cover them with fresh greaseproof paper and foil and store them in a cool dry cupboard. They will be all the better for maturing. The cake is also best made around this time, although it must not be iced until much later. To store, wrap the cake in greaseproof paper and then foil and keep it in an airtight tin;

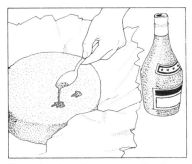

Spooning brandy over stored cake

unwrap it every couple of weeks or so, prick it with a fine skewer and spoon a little brandy over it.

USING THE FREEZER
If you have a freezer you can start, any time from November onwards, to build up stocks of foods which you know will be wanted. Pastry freezes well, so

make mince pies, sausage rolls and flan cases. Two or three un-decorated sponge cakes, for turning into gâteaux or trifles, could form part of your planned Boxing Day menu; otherwise they make good standbys for when you have more guests than you expected. Meringues, brandy snaps, short-bread and biscuits will also be useful. Do make a list, though, of what you are putting in the freezer. It is surprising how you can forget what you have in there.

Don't just freeze party foods either. In the pre-Christmas rush of carol services, parties, shopping and decorating the tree, there are bound to be days when cooking is one chore too many. If, during November, you lay in a few family casseroles and soups, you will heave a sigh of relief on hectic days later.

For Christmas Day itself there are lots of small things you can freeze to make life easier at the last minute. Cranberry sauce and apple sauce freeze well, and so does brandy butter for the mince pies. Make up little bags of bread-crumbs for stuffing and bread sauce—or make the sauce and stuffing completely. If you make

Shaping stuffing into small balls

the stuffing in advance, shape it into small balls for easy cooking. Béchamel sauce is useful too; freeze it in small quantities.

Finally, when you take the turkey out, fill the space it leaves with bread and rolls.

SHOPPING AHEAD

Shopping is a chore that gets more difficult the nearer you get to Christmas. Stores become more and more crowded, the shelves empty more quickly, transport becomes more of a problem due to volume of traffic (and often bad weather), and even the bags seem to conspire to be heavier. So do what you can before the start of the Christmas rush.

Anything that can be frozen or that comes in a can or packet can be bought early. Check your stocks of standard frozen foods — things like puff pastry, peas and oven chips, ice cream and beefburgers. These are not special Christmas foods, but they will still be wanted. Buy them early so that you only have to think about fresh foods at the last moment.

Dry stores like flour and sugar, coffee, tea and breakfast cereals, will keep quite adequately for a month or so — get that shopping out of the way too. Many non-food items are bulky and difficult to carry; shop early for foil, cling film, absorbent kitchen paper, greaseproof paper, paper napkins, toilet paper, washing-up liquid and dishwasher detergent. And if you stock up with pet food you won't find yourself feeding turkey to your pet.

INVITATIONS

If you are having a party between Christmas and the New Year, invitations need to be out by the first week in December. In some areas it is immensely difficult to shop between 24th December and 2nd January, so you have to be able to plan and order in advance.

If you have some idea of numbers by the end of the second week in December, you can then buy in wines, beer and spirits, soft drinks and all the crisps, nuts and nibbles you need.

ORDER EARLY

Any large items that form a major part of your menu over the holiday should be ordered well in advance. This applies particularly to meats. Order the turkey or goose to ensure you can have one the size you require, plus any joints of ham, beef or pork, including joints for the New Year. If you order sausages and streaky bacon at the same time you will be sure of having all the trimmings you want. If you want a salted tongue or beef joint, the butcher will need to know in order to brine it.

Bread, milk, cream and yogurt should also be ordered. But it is generally better not to order vegetables and fruit. With produce that is so susceptible to weather conditions, you will do better to turn up yourself 1–2 days before Christmas, without too many firm ideas about what you are going to buy. Select your purchases according to what is freshest and best — and you will be sure of eating well.

DECORATING THE CAKE

Ice and decorate the Christmas cake in stages through December, aiming to be finished about a week before Christmas. That will give the icing time to set properly but not to harden unpleasantly.

If you are decorating the cake formally, with a base of flat icing plus piping, start by applying the almond paste in the first week of December. Leave it to dry for 4–5 days before adding icing, other-wise the yellow almond oils will leech into the icing and spoil the pure white colour. The first coat of flat icing should then be allowed to dry for 2 days before you add the second. Then leave piping and any moulded trim-mings until, at the most, a week before Christmas.

Rough icing, to make a tradi-tional snow scene, is done all in

one go. So you can start a little later. Put on the almond paste about 10 days before Christmas, leave it to dry for 4–5 days then finish off with icing.

A cake that is coated with almond paste and royal icing is well sealed from the air and will not go stale quickly, so once you have started decorating there is no need to worry about an airtight tin. If the cake is too large to go in

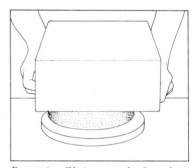

Protecting Christmas cake from dust

a tin, just leave it on its board with a tin inverted over it to keep off the dust; or wrap it lightly in a large polythene bag, leaving the end open so that it does not sweat. Alternatively, a loose wrapping of foil would serve the same purpose.

There is no way you can avoid a rush at the last minute, but if these major preparations are out of the way, at least you will feel that you have things under control.

THE BIRD

Poultry is not only traditional for Christmas, it is economical. A big turkey feeds a lot of people and is as tasty cold as hot.

Of course, if you are cooking for one or two a chicken is much more sensible and you can still have all the trimmings, but it is much more fun when numbers are small to go for something more out of the ordinary. Goose and duck are seasonal birds that give a really 'old-fashioned' feel to the Christmas meal. A 1.8–2.2 kg (4–5 lb) duck serves 4; a 4.5 kg (10 lb) goose serves 6–8. The meat from these birds is very rich and is not as popular cold as turkey or chicken.

When buying turkey, use the following chart as a guide. All weights given are for oven-ready birds; if buying your bird undressed, add about 1.4 kg (3 lb) to the weight.

Oven-ready weight	Servings
2.7–3.5 kg (6–8 lb)	6–10
4.5–5.9 kg (10–13 lb)	12–20
6.5–9 kg (14–20 lb)	20–30

It is useful to know that a 4.5 kg (10 lb) turkey yields about 2.4 kg (5 lb 8 oz) meat. As a straight roast meal, with the trimmings, this will serve 8, plus a further 4 servings as cold cuts, and should leave you enough for a réchauffé dish for 4 as well.

THAWING

All frozen poultry must be completely thawed before cooking. This should be done at a room temperature of 16°–17°C (65°–70°F), in the bag. Thawing in the refrigerator or at lower temperatures is too slow to be safe. Remove the giblets and neck as soon as they are free and use them for making stock for gravy.

Remember that once thawed, poultry becomes as perishable as any fresh meat and should be cooked as soon as possible.

Approximate thawing times at room temperature

1.4 kg (3 lb)	9 hours
2.3 kg (5 lb)	15 hours
4.5 kg (10 lb)	18 hours
6.8 kg (15 lb)	24 hours
9 kg (20 lb)	30 hours

STUFFING

When estimating stuffing quantities, allow about 225 g (8 oz) for each 2.3 kg (5 lb) of turkey. Mix the stuffing in advance if you want, but don't put it in to the bird until immediately before cooking. Then stuff the neck cavity only, not too tightly.

COOKING TIMES

Always weigh the bird after you have stuffed it.
Turkey: Brush the bird all over with melted butter or oil and cover

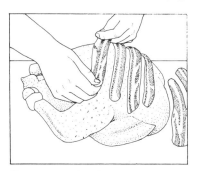

Covering poultry breast with bacon

the breast with strips of streaky bacon if you wish. Place in a roasting tin and roast at 180°C (350°F) mark 4 for 20 minutes per 450 g (1 lb), plus an extra 20 minutes. Put a piece of foil over the breast towards the end of the cooking time if it shows signs of becoming too brown.
Goose: Place in a roasting tin and cover the breast with foil. Roast at 200°C (400°F) mark 6 for 15

minutes per 450 g (1 lb), plus an extra 15 minutes. Baste the bird frequently during cooking and remove the foil for the last 20 minutes so that the breast can brown.
Duckling: Prick the skin all over with a fork and place the bird on a wire rack in a roasting tin. Roast uncovered at 180°C (350°F) mark 4, allowing 30–35 minutes per 450 g (1 lb).

BONING A TURKEY

If you plan to serve your Christmas turkey as the centre-piece of a buffet, it may be boned, stuffed and cooked ahead of time, with no last minute fuss.

To bone a turkey, cut off the wings at the second joint, the legs at the first and remove the parson's nose. Lay the bird on its breast, cut straight down the back through the skin to the bone. Keeping the knife close to the carcass, gradually ease flesh and skin away from the bone. Work down towards the joints, turning the bird as you go.

Clasping one leg in each hand, press very firmly outwards to release the leg joints. Ease the point of the knife into the joints and separate the legs from the body. Repeat for the wings.

Return to the main body and continue carefully filleting the flesh from the breast bone. Work down both sides of the bone and along the tip until the whole carcass can be removed.

Holding the thigh end of the leg joint, scrape all the flesh from the thigh. Cut carefully round the joint with the point of the knife and scrape the drumstick clean in the same way. Pull leg completely inside out to remove the bone, snipping any sinews. Repeat with the other leg. Remove the wings similarly and remove the wishbone.

PREPARING FOR THE CHRISTMAS LUNCH

Have in your mind a rota of helpers for Christmas Day. They needn't know what you have in store, but if all the family and any visitors do just a little, your day will be easier without spoiling theirs.

CHRISTMAS EVE

Shopping: Check all your lists and do, or send someone else out for, the final shopping.

Turkey: Is the turkey thawing steadily? If not, move it to a slightly warmer atmosphere. As soon as you can remove the giblets from a frozen turkey, or as soon as you are ready with a fresh one, simmer them with flavouring vegetables to make stock for the gravy.

Sauces: Take stuffings, sauces and brandy butter out of the freezer to thaw. Or prepare fresh what you haven't frozen and store in the refrigerator.

Vegetables: Persuade someone to trim green vegetables and peel carrots. Leave them in a cool place. Do not wash greens until just before cooking as the extra water will encourage them to turn soft. Potatoes for roasting can be

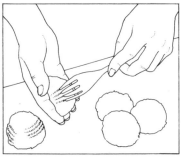

Scratching surface for crisp potatoes

peeled and parboiled. Scratch the dry surfaces to make them extra crisp when cooked.

Desserts: Make and chill any cold desserts. Prepare fruit salads but do not add black grapes or bananas. Grapes can be halved and pipped but will leech their colour when added to the syrup; bananas need to be peeled and sliced into the syrup just before serving otherwise they discolour and go soft. Make the cake and custard base for a trifle, but don't add cream until shortly before serving. If you are going to have a starter, choose something simple—smoked salmon, melon with port, or a fresh fruit and vegetable salad. Alternatively, make a pâté ahead of time and freeze it. Take it out of the freezer and refrigerate overnight.

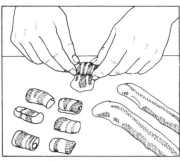

Bacon rolls can be made in advance

Trimmings for the roast: Prick sausages and make bacon rolls. Lay them in a baking tin, cover and put in the refrigerator or cold place overnight. Before you go to bed, take dripping or butter out of the refrigerator to soften. Work out roughly what time you need to start cooking next day (see page 137 for turkey cooking times).

It is best, if possible, also to lay the table on Christmas Eve.

Christmas Day (for lunch at 1.00 pm)

Early morning: Turn on the oven to preheat. Stuff the turkey, truss it and spread with soft dripping or butter, or brush with oil or melted butter. Add strips of bacon over the breast if you wish. Weigh the prepared turkey and calculate the cooking time (see page 137). Then add an extra 30 minutes; this allows time for the turkey to stand,

making it easier to carve, and gives you time to make gravy.

At the calculated time, put the bird to cook.

Finish any cold desserts, appetisers and sauces. Take mince pies out of the freezer.

10.00 am Put the pudding on to steam. Lay the table if you haven't already done so and prepare the wines. Put plates and serving dishes to warm.

11.30 am Heat dripping and put the potatoes to roast. Bring the cheese into the kitchen to 'come to' at room temperature. Put sausages and bacon rolls to cook alongside the potatoes. Reheat sauces and keep them warm in a bain-marie.

12.00 pm If serving a salad as a starter, dress it. Arrange the starter on individual plates.

12.30 pm The turkey should be cooked. Check, and if it is, cook the vegetables, starting with those that take longest; drain and keep hot. Transfer the bird to a carving dish, return to the oven at its lowest setting and keep warm while you make the gravy. If serving a large number of people, carve in the kitchen so that you can keep individual portions hot. For smaller numbers, garnish the bird ready to take to the table whole.

Turn the pudding out on to a serving plate, but leave covered with the basin; leave in the oven to keep hot.

Dish up and cover the vegetables; keep them hot while you serve the starter.

Put the mince pies in the oven to reheat on low, when you serve the main course.

LEFTOVERS

When using up leftovers there are two basic rules to remember. The first is always to add some fresh ingredient to the one that has been previously cooked. A meal consisting entirely of leftovers cannot fail to be dull; the new ingredient adds sparkle to the old. The second rule is to beware of overcooking. Food that has been cooked once does not need cooking again—merely reheating. Once the dish is heated through, it should be served at once.

Here are some ideas for using up your Christmas leftovers.

SPICED TURKEY AND BEAN RAGOÛT

Serves 8

100 g (4 oz) butter or margarine

2 medium onions, skinned and roughly chopped

60 ml (4 tbsp) plain flour

15 ml (1 tbsp) Chilli Seasoning

793 g (1 lb 12 oz) can tomatoes

30 ml (2 tbsp) Worcestershire sauce

60 ml (4 tbsp) tomato purée

900 ml (1½ pints) chicken or turkey stock

15 ml (1 tbsp) caster sugar

2 bay leaves

salt and freshly ground pepper

700–900 g (1½–2 lb) cooked turkey meat, cut into large dice

400 g (14 oz) can sweet red peppers (pimientos), drained

432 g (15¼ oz) can red kidney beans, drained

1 Melt 50 g (2 oz) of the butter in a heavy-based saucepan, add the onion and fry for about 5 minutes until golden. Stir in the flour and Chilli Seasoning, then continue frying for 2 minutes.

2 Add the tomatoes with their juice, the Worcestershire sauce, tomato purée, stock, sugar, bay leaves and salt and pepper to taste. Bring to the boil, cover then simmer for 30 minutes.

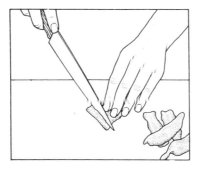

3 Dice the pimiento. Melt the remaining butter in a frying pan and fry the turkey for 5 minutes.

4 Stir the turkey, diced pimiento and beans into the sauce and simmer for a further 10 minutes. Serve immediately.

DEEP DISH TURKEY PIE

Serves 4

350 g (12 oz) cooked turkey meat

225 g (8 oz) stuffing from the turkey

2 oranges

25 g (1 oz) butter or margarine

1 medium onion, skinned and finely chopped

30 ml (2 tbsp) plain flour

200 ml (7 fl oz) dry cider

salt and freshly ground pepper

368 g (13 oz) packet frozen puff pastry, thawed

beaten egg, to glaze

1 Cut the turkey into large bite-sized pieces and place in a 1.1 litre (2 pint) pie dish with a pie funnel placed in the centre.

2 Roll the stuffing into 8 even-sized balls and place on top of the turkey.

3 Peel the oranges and divide into segments, removing all pith. Add to the dish.

4 Melt the butter in a saucepan, add the onion and fry gently for about 5 minutes until golden. Add the flour and cook gently, stirring, for 1–2 minutes.

5 Gradually blend in the cider and bring to the boil, stirring. Season and pour into the pie dish.

6 Roll out the pastry on a floured surface and cover the pie with it. Glaze with beaten egg and bake at 200°C (400°F) mark 6 for about 35 minutes or until well browned. Serve hot.

IDEAS FOR LEFTOVER HAM

Ham Dip: Mix finely chopped cooked ham with soured cream, mayonnaise, Worcestershire sauce and salt. Serve with crudités and crisps.

Glazed Kebabs: Thread chunks of cooked ham and thick wedges of apple alternately on to skewers. Brush with marmalade mixed with lemon juice and grill until glazed.

Ham and Watercress Soup: Bring well-flavoured chicken stock to the boil, add a few sliced mushrooms, slivers of cooked ham and trimmed watercress sprigs. Bring back to the boil, season with salt and pepper to taste and serve immediately.

Ham Casserole: Mix drained, canned red kidney beans with tomato ketchup, brown sugar, mustard, diced green pepper and chunks of cooked ham; bake until heated through.

Decorating the Christmas Cake and Festive Drinks

A rich fruit cake is part of the traditional British way of celebrating Christmas. Laden with dried fruits and laced with brandy, the inside is often almost black. Outside, the white icing is decorated not with images of the Christ child but with scenes or symbols connected with the Santa Claus legend. Sprigs of holly, snow, reindeer or small models of Santa are usually part of the decoration.
To make the cake, follow the recipe on page 95.
For around the Christmas period, there are also suggestions for hot and cold drinks.

APRICOT GLAZE

Makes 150 ml ($\frac{1}{4}$ pint)

100 g (4 oz) apricot preserve

1 Put the apricot preserve and 30 ml (2 tbsp) water in a saucepan and heat gently, stirring, until the preserve softens. Bring to the boil and simmer for 1 minute.

2 Use the glaze while still warm (see steps 4 and 6 of Applying Almond Paste).

ALMOND PASTE

Makes about 450 g (1 lb)

100 g (4 oz) icing sugar

100 g (4 oz) caster sugar

225 g (8 oz) ground almonds

2.5 ml ($\frac{1}{2}$ tsp) vanilla flavouring

15–30 ml (1–2 tbsp) lemon juice

1 egg, beaten

1 Sift the icing sugar into a bowl and stir in the caster sugar and ground almonds.

2 Add the flavouring and 15 ml (1 tbsp) lemon juice, then work in the egg with more lemon juice if needed to form a stiff paste. Form into a ball and knead lightly.

APPLYING ALMOND PASTE

1 Measure round the cake with a piece of string. Dust the working surface with icing sugar.

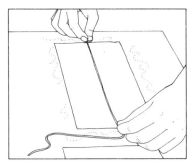

2 Roll out two-thirds of the paste to a rectangle, half the length of the string by twice the depth of the cake.

3 Trim the rectangle and cut in half lengthways.

4 Place the cake upside down on a board and brush the sides with apricot glaze.

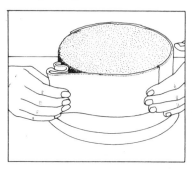

5 Gently lift the almond paste and place it firmly in position round the cake. Smooth the joins with a palette knife and keep the top and bottom edges square. Roll a jam jar lightly round the cake to help the paste stick more firmly.

6 Brush the top of the cake with apricot glaze and roll out the remaining almond paste to fit.

7 With the help of the rolling pin, lift it carefully on to the cake. Lightly roll with the rolling pin, then smooth the join and leave to dry for 2–5 days before starting to ice.

ROYAL ICING

Makes about 450 g (1 lb)

2 egg whites
450 g (1 lb) icing sugar
5 ml (1 tsp) lemon juice
5 ml (1 tsp) glycerine

1 Whisk the egg whites in a bowl until slightly frothy. Sift and stir in about a quarter of the icing sugar with a wooden spoon. Continue adding more sugar gradually, beating well after each addition, until about three-quarters of the sugar has been added altogether.

2 Beat in the lemon juice and continue beating for about 10 minutes until the icing is smooth.

3 Beat in the remaining sugar until the required consistency is achieved, depending on how the icing will be used.

4 Finally, stir in the glycerine to prevent the icing hardening. Cover and keep for 24 hours to allow air bubbles to rise to the surface.

ICING A CAKE

Always apply royal icing over a layer of almond paste rather than directly on to the cake.

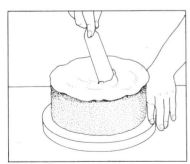

1 Stand the cake and board on a non-slip surface. Spoon almost half the icing on to the top of the cake and spread it evenly over the surface with a palette knife, using a paddling action.

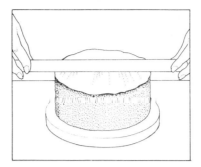

2 Using an icing ruler or palette knife longer than the width of the cake, without applying any pressure, draw it steadily across the top of the cake at an angle of 30°. Repeat if necessary.

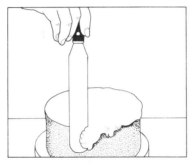

3 Neaten the edges by holding a palette knife upright and running it around the rim of the cake to remove surplus icing. Leave to dry for about 24 hours before applying icing to side of cake. Cover remaining icing.

4 Place cake on an icing turn-table or upturned plate. Spread remaining icing on the side and smooth roughly with a small palette knife, using a paddling action as for the top of the cake.

5 Hold the palette knife upright and at an angle of 45° to the cake. Draw the knife or comb towards you to smooth the surface. For a square cake, apply icing to each side separately. Neaten the edges with a palette knife. Reserve the surplus icing for decorating.

6 For a really smooth finish, allow to dry for 1–2 days, then thin icing with a little water, and apply this as a second coat. Use a sharp knife to trim off any rough icing. Use sandpaper to sand down any imperfections in the first coat. Brush surface with greasefree pastry brush to remove icing dust. Leave to dry thoroughly before adding piped decorations.

MOULDED ICING

Makes about 450 g (1 lb)

450 g (1 lb) icing sugar
1 egg white
50 g (2 oz) liquid glucose
colouring
flavouring

1 Sift the icing sugar into a mixing bowl and make a well in the centre. Add the egg white and glucose. Beat, gradually draw-ing the icing sugar into the centre of the bowl, until the mixture is quite stiff. Knead the icing, incorporating any remaining icing sugar, until smooth and manage-able. Add colouring and flavour-ing and a little more icing sugar if necessary. Store the icing in a sealed polythene bag or container in a cool place to prevent it drying.

To Use the Icing to Cover a Cake

Roll out the icing to a round or square 5 cm (2 inches) larger than the cake. Lift the icing on the rolling pin and place on top of the marzipan-covered cake. Press the icing on to the side of the cake, working the surplus to the base. Lightly dust your hands in icing sugar and rub the top and sides in a circular movement to make it smooth. Cut off the surplus icing at the base.

CHRISTMAS TREE CAKE

Make the cake itself well in advance to give the flavour time to mature, and feed it with brandy from time to time.

Aim to complete the decorating about a week before Christmas. Once iced, the cake will keep fresh without an airtight tin, but protect it by covering it with a cake dome or an upturned box.

Christmas cake (page 95)

apricot glaze (page 140)

450 g (1 lb) almond paste (page 140)

450 g (1 lb) royal icing (page 141)

green and red food colouring

silver balls, wide red ribbon and thin green ribbon, to decorate

1 Between 14 and 20 days before required, place the cake on a 23 cm (9 inch) cake board. Brush with apricot glaze and cover with almond paste (page 140). Loosely cover the cake and store in a cool dry place for 4–5 days.

2 Using the royal icing, flat ice the top (page 141). Leave to dry for about 24 hours before icing the sides.

3 Using the royal icing, ice the sides of the cake (page 141). Leave to dry for 1–2 days, then apply the second coat, if necessary.

4 Meanwhile, prepare the decorations and leave to dry for 24 hours. Colour most of the remaining almond paste dark green and a small piece red using food colouring.

5 Draw the outline of a Christmas tree on a piece of card and cut out with sharp scissors.

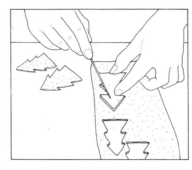

6 Roll out the green almond paste on a piece of non-stick paper and, using the Christmas tree template, cut out 4–6 trees.

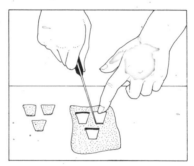

7 Roll out the red almond paste and cut to make 4–6 tub shapes for the tree bases.

8 Attach the trees to the bases and position a silver ball at each point. Leave to dry, then fix on cake with icing.

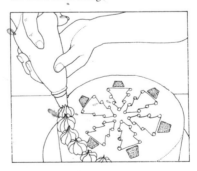

9 Using an icing bag fitted with an 8-point star nozzle and filled with royal icing, pipe a border around top edge of cake.

10 Place a silver ball in the centre of every other piped star before the icing dries.

11 Using the same icing bag and nozzle as for the top edge, pipe a shell border along the base edge of the cake.

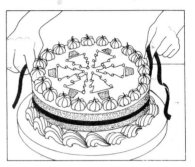

12 Place the wide red ribbon around the cake and secure the ends with headed pins. Lay the narrow green ribbon over the wide ribbon, making sure it is central, then secure.

ALTERNATIVE DECORATIONS

Holly, berries and ivy leaves
For holly leaves, colour some almond paste dark green by kneading in a few drops of green food colouring. Roll out evenly on a piece of non-stick or waxed paper. Cut into small rectangles and then cut into a holly leaf shape using the base of an icing nozzle. Mark in the centre vein with a knife and leave until dry.

For berries, colour some almond paste red and roll into small balls.

For ivy leaves, colour some almond paste light green and roll out as above. Cut out the leaf shape freehand and mark with veins then leave to dry.

DRINKS

Along with the food, the alcohol flows freely over the Christmas season. You will need wines for dinner and buffet parties, aperitifs and shorts for people who drop in casually. And if the weather is seasonally cold, nothing can beat a hot punch or mulled wine.

GUIDE TO QUANTITIES

Only you know how much your friends drink, and how generous you wish to be with the alcohol. But the following guide will give you a helping hand when planning and stocking up. Remember always to have soft drinks on hand as well, for those who are not taking alcohol, and make these as interesting as possible—just because somebody is driving home doesn't mean they should be given plain orange squash!

Wine: For Christmas lunch and buffet parties, allow 1–2 aperitifs or shorts and half a bottle of wine per person.
Drop-in-for-drinks: Allow 3–5 short drinks each. Some people prefer to drink a glass of wine or beer—an opened bottle of white wine will keep in the refrigerator for a day or two.

DRINKS BY THE BOTTLE
Sherry, port and vermouth give roughly 12–16 glasses per bottle. In single nips for cocktails, vermouths and spirits give just over 30 a bottle. Reckon 16–20 drinks of spirit from a bottle when serving them with soda, tonic or other minerals. Liqueurs (served in proper liqueur glasses) give 30 portions per bottle. A 700 ml (20 fl oz) bottle of tonic or soda gives 2–3 drinks; 600 ml (1 pint) tomato juice gives 4–6 drinks.

JULGLÖGG (SWEDISH CHRISTMAS WINE)
Serves about 12

1 bottle of aquavit or gin
2 bottles of Burgundy wine
75 g (3 oz) seedless raisins
100 g (4 oz) granulated sugar
15 ml (1 tbsp) cardamom seeds
6 cloves
5 cm (2 inch) cinnamon stick
small piece of lemon rind

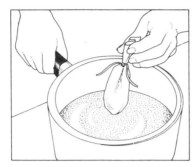

1 Pour half the aquavit or gin into a saucepan with the wine. Add the raisins and sugar. Tie the spices and lemon rind in muslin and add to the pan. Cover and bring very slowly to the boil. Simmer for 30 minutes.

2 Add the remaining aquavit or gin and remove from the heat. Take out the spices and, just before serving, ignite the punch. Serve in tumblers or punch glasses.

DUBONNET ALMOND PUNCH
Serves 6

3 thin-skinned oranges
75 cl bottle red Dubonnet
150 ml (¼ pint) Amaretto liqueur
12 allspice berries
6 cloves

1 Peel and thinly slice 1 of the oranges. Put in saucepan with the remaining ingredients. Heat almost to boiling point.

2 Squeeze the juice from the remaining oranges and add to the punch with 600 ml (1 pint) boiling water. Serve hot.

GLÜHWEIN (AUSTRIAN MULLED RED WINE)
Serves about 4

4 cloves
1 lemon
600 ml (1 pint) red wine
75 g (3 oz) brown sugar
two 5 cm (2 inch) cinnamon sticks
150 ml (¼ pint) brandy

1 Push the cloves into the lemon and put in a saucepan with the wine, sugar and cinnamon.

2 Bring to simmering point and simmer gently, covered, for 2–4 minutes.

3 Remove from the heat, add the brandy, strain and serve at once.

SPICY FRUIT PUNCH
Makes about 25 wine glasses

100 g (4 oz) granulated sugar
1 litre (35.2 fl oz) carton orange juice
two 200 ml (7.05 fl oz) cartons unsweetened pineapple juice
pared rind and juice of 1 lemon
2.5 ml (½ tsp) grated nutmeg
2.5 ml (½ tsp) mixed spice
6 cloves
two 500 ml (17.6 fl oz) bottles ginger ale
2 oranges, sliced, to garnish

1 Over a low heat dissolve the sugar in 600 ml (1 pint) water. Add the fruit juices, lemon rind and juice and spices. Heat until the mixture is almost boiling.

2 Add the ginger ale and reheat. Strain into a serving bowl and garnish with orange slices.

Preserving

Fruit preserves and relishes, fruit-flavoured brandies and rich confectionery are all part of the Christmas tradition. Bringing the flavours of summer to mid-winter, they add the finishing touch to well thought-out party meals and also make delightful presents. Pot chutneys and conserves in pretty jars, making decorative labels if they are intended as gifts. For confectionery, go to town with neat boxes and seasonal wrappings.

The discovery of sugar and alcohol as preservatives must surely go down among the 'finds' of all time. Certainly drying, bottling and freezing are all methods of preserving, giving long lasting and versatile results, but caramelled fruits and fruits steeped in alcohol come into the class of luxury foods.

CHOOSING FRUITS FOR STEEPING IN ALCOHOL

It is only worth preserving best-quality fruits. Anything else will give disappointing results. The fruit should be ripe but firm and free from blemishes. Soft fruits are not suitable for steeping in alcohol, but they make excellent jams and conserves.

Pricking small fruit before preserving

Small fruits that are to be preserved whole in alcohol should be pricked all over so that the syrup can penetrate the skin, larger fruits such as peaches or pears should be peeled and halved, with the stones or cores removed.

SUGAR

Granulated sugar is suitable for all kinds of preserving, and is certainly the cheapest to use. But for a really clear jelly or sparkling conserve, choose preserving sugar. It makes less scum as it boils and the colour of the fruit will show through more brightly.

Brown sugar is equally good as a preservative, but it will darken a jam considerably and the molasses flavour may overpower that of the fruit. In mincemeat, brown sugar is excellent; a dark, rich colour is what most people want, and the possible variations of flavour can be exciting.

CANDIED PEEL, CARAMELLED FRUITS AND CRYSTALLISED FLOWERS

Candied fruit is expensive to buy, not because of exotic ingredients but because the process is fiddly and can take anything from two to three weeks. Candied peel is made in much the same way, but is quicker and easier (page 150). Caramelled fruit is easier still, as are crystallised flower petals and crystallised leaves.

STORING PRESERVES

JELLIES, CONSERVES AND MINCEMEAT

After spooning into clean dry jars, the surface of the preserve should

Covering preserve with waxed paper

be covered with a disc of waxed paper. Press the waxed side of the paper firmly against the preserve, taking it right to the sides of the jar so that air is excluded as far as possible. Then cover with a Cellophane disc held in place with a rubber band, or with a screw top. Store the jars in a cool, dry, dark place. Warmth or damp may cause fermentation or mould growth; light spoils the colour of jams and jellies.

CHUTNEYS

The vinegar in chutney evaporates all too readily so this type of preserve needs a stronger covering than waxed paper. Choose jars with glass stoppers or plastic screw lids (not metal, the vinegar will corrode it quickly).

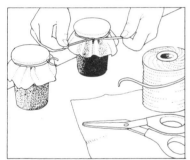

'Preserving skin' for covering home-made chutney

Alternatively, buy "preserving skin", cut it to shape and tie firmly in place with string, or use corks dipped in paraffin wax.

Again choose a cool, dry, dark place for storage. Chutney ferments quickly in a warm kitchen.

MAKING SWEETS

Many sweets can be made simply, without cooking. Care in shaping and pretty presentation are all that is required for spectacular results. But for many types of confectionery, the sugar must be boiled—the final temperature of the syrup governing the texture of the finished sweet.

The most accurate way of test-ing the sugar temperature is with a thermometer. Choose one that is easy to read and graduates from 16°C (60°F) to 182°C (360°F) or 232°C (450°F). Thermometers are

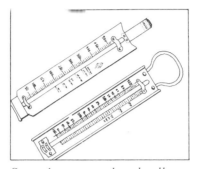

Sugar thermometers have handles or clips

usually mounted on stainless steel or brass and may have either a brass or wooden handle, or a sliding clip that can be fixed to the edge of the pan. Season a new thermometer by placing it in cold water, bringing the pan to the boil and leaving it in the water to cool. Check what it reads when the water is boiling to see that it is accurate. It should read 100°C (212°F).

Warm a thermometer before dipping it in hot sugar, or the sudden heat may crack it. While you are not using it, stand the thermometer in a jug of hot water. When you have finished with it, clean the thermometer very thoroughly as any sugar crystals left on it could spoil the reading next time you use it.

If you do not have a thermometer, it is possible to

Testing temperature of sugar

check the temperature of the syrup by dropping a small amount into cold water. The appearance when it cools is your guide to tem-perature. Always remove the pan from the heat while testing in case it goes past the point you want.

SAUCEPANS

Pans for sweet making should be strong and thick-based to prevent burning and sticking. Non-stick pans are not suitable as the high temperature may damage the lining; enamel is also liable to damage, so choose aluminium, stainless steel, copper or brass. Always choose a high-sided pan, much larger than you think you might need at first sight—when boiling, sugar rises very high up the sides of the pan and may be dangerous if allowed to boil over.

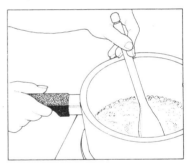

Use a long-handled spoon to stir sugar when sweet-making

STIRRING

Use a long-handled wooden spoon to stir the sugar, keeping your hand well clear of any splashes. For most sweets, stir until the sugar is dissolved, then boil with-out stirring until the required temperature is reached. With fudges, this is difficult; the milk, butter or cream used encourages the mixture to stick to the pan, so you must stir occasionally to prevent it sticking and burning. But stir only as much as is absolutely necessary.

TESTS FOR BOILING SUGAR

These are the most important stages in sugar boiling.
Smooth: 102°–104°C (215°–220°F). Used for crystallising. The mixture looks syrupy. To test, dip

Syrup clings to the fingers at the smooth stage

your fingers in water and then very quickly in the syrup. Your thumb will slide smoothly over your fingers, but the syrup will cling to them.
Soft ball: 116°–118°C (240°–245°F). Used for fondants and fudges. Using a spoon, drop a

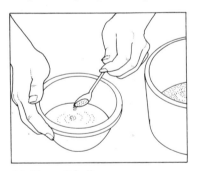

Making soft ball test

little of the syrup into a bowl of chilled water. Then pick it up with your fingers and see if it will form a soft ball. At 116°C (240°F) the ball will flatten when you take it out of the water; the higher the temperature, the firmer the ball.
Firm or hard ball: 120°–130°C (250°–265°F). Used for caramels. When dropped into cold water the syrup forms a ball that is hard enough to hold its shape, though still pliable.

Soft crack: 132°–143°C (270°–290°F). Used for toffees. When dropped into cold water the syrup separates into threads that are hard but not brittle.
Hard crack: 149°–154°C (300°–310°F). Used for hard toffees. When dropped into cold water the syrup forms hard, brittle threads.

STORING SWEETS

Home-made sweets should be stored in a cool place in tightly covered containers. Uncooked sweets and unboiled marzipan do not keep well—use within a week. Toffees and caramels should be wrapped in cling film to prevent them going soft. Different types of sweets should be stored separately until you are ready to gift wrap or serve them, to prevent flavours mixing.

Chocolates are best covered with cling film and stored in an airtight tin. Don't keep them long or they will lose their gloss. Truffles and chocolates with a high percentage of cream in them should be stored in the refrigerator.

Once fudge has been cut, store it between sheets of waxed paper in an airtight tin. It will keep for up to 2–3 weeks.

PACKING SWEETS FOR GIFTS

Some sweets need to be wrapped individually, just to keep them in good condition, even if you are not planning to give them away. So start with these basic wrappings, leaving gift wrappings until the last minute so that they are totally fresh and sparkling on the day. Use Cellophane, cling film, foil or waxed paper to wrap boiled sweets or toffees, caramels and nougat. Square and oblong sweets can be done up in neat parcels, or the

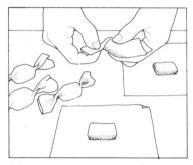

Wrapping rounds and cushions

paper can be twisted in opposite directions at each end—this is the way to deal with rounds and cushions.

Then for gift boxes you might try over-wrapping with metallic paper in gold, silver or colours. These can look really luxurious, but mix your colours with restraint to avoid cheapening the appearance. Sweets that don't need wrapping are best placed in paper sweet cases—brown for chocolates, or patterned, or gold or silver foil.

Store wrapped and cased sweets in a shallow tin until ready to gift pack. Take care not to damage them by piling them on top of each other.

BOX OR BAG?

Choose your gift packaging according to the type of sweet. Toffees, caramels and most hard sweets can be packed in bags. You

Various packaging for home-made sweets as gifts

can make these in the shape of a cone or dolly bag, a simple wrap-over bag or even a Christmas cracker. Fondants, creams and chocolates need the protection of a rigid container.

BOUGHT BOXES

Many gift shops and stationers sell pretty gift boxes in varying shapes, sizes and colours. These make very effective packaging for home-made sweets, needing only a tie of gold thread or ribbon to finish them off. But shallow trays are hard to come by; if you buy

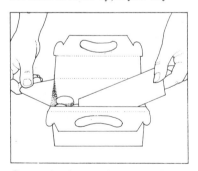

Separating layers of sweets with card

deeper boxes that will take the sweets in several layers, do separate the layers with squares of card to protect delicate sweets. Brightly coloured miniature carrier bags are also available; these are pretty and inexpensive

but give no protection, so they are really only suitable for hard sweets.

RECYCLED CONTAINERS

Using containers you already have around the house is much cheaper, and can look equally good if you trim them carefully. The first rule here is never to use any container that has held perfumed goods such as soap—the smell will quickly contaminate the sweets. Any surface marks that tell of previous uses are less important; they are easily covered.

A small carton that has held tea bags or after-dinner mints is ideal for home-made sweets. This is the easiest and quickest way of making a professional-looking box.

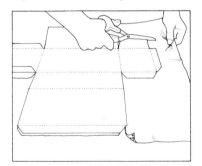

Covering carton with paper

Open it out carefully, taking care not to tear it where it was stuck, and lay it out flat. Dab a very little adhesive all over the outside and place a sheet of wrapping paper on top; smooth it out gently and press firmly in place. If the paper has a distinctive design, make sure the motifs fall centrally on the box. Cut the paper accurately to match the edges of the carton after it is stuck.

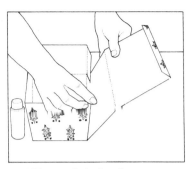

Refolding and glueing the carton

Then turn the carton over and line the inside of the lid in the same way, either using the same paper or a toning plain paper. Now re-fold the box along the crease lines and glue the sides where appropriate.

Before putting the sweets in the box, line it with fresh waxed paper or a paper doily. Dark waxed paper, which can be bought from specialist suppliers, is best for chocolates as it does not show marks; or a gold doily can look dramatic.

Used toffee tins, or tins that have held cocoa, coffee or drinking chocolate also make good sweet containers. Start by washing and drying them thoroughly. Then paint the outside, using either an aerosol spray or a brush-on acrylic paint. Mask the inside with crumpled paper if using a spray. You may need several coats to cover the surface adequately, then

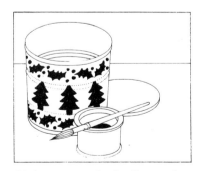

Make pretty packaging from used tins by painting them

patterns can be stencilled or hand painted on the sides. Or glue on braid or paper cut-outs to trim.

If you prefer, you can cover the tins with wrapping paper or sticky-backed shelf paper. Don't forget to paint or cover the lid as well; an airtight seal is good for the hard sweets you can store in these tins.

Glass jars display sweets effectively

Glass storage jars make lovely gift containers for sweets. They look neat, display the sweets prettily, and the recipient has something usable left after the contents are all eaten. A shiny ribbon is all the trimming needed. Other suitable re-usable containers include individual mugs or glasses or pretty cups and saucers. When filled, cover with cling film.

CHOCOLATE BOXES

The containers mentioned so far are mostly deep, and suitable for robust sweets only. Delicate chocolates, marzipan petits fours and candied fruits need a shallow container with rigid sides, in which they can sit prettily in a single layer.

Foil freezer trays make pretty packaging for these. A shallow flan dish or foil baking tin can be lined

Foil tins are perfect for chocolates

with coloured tissue or a doily and covered with cling film or cellophane. Tie round the outside with a bright ribbon or braid, and add a ribbon bow for a really 'complete' look. Shallow plastic containers, paper plates or oven-proof paper dishes are also good.

MAKING YOUR OWN BOXES

If the idea of re-using an old chocolate box doesn't appeal, you can nevertheless use it as a guide to making your own.

To make a box, buy lightweight coloured card from an art shop. Open out the used box carefully, taking care not to tear the tabs and fold-over corners. Lay this opened-out box on the new card and draw round it as a guide. Cut out the shape with scissors.

Before you go on, experiment with a spare piece of card and a scalpel or DIY knife until you can score the fold lines accurately, without cutting right through.

Working on a hard surface such as a chopping board or the back of an old wooden tray, score along all the fold lines with a scalpel and straight edge. Fold carefully along the scored lines, lightly glueing the tabs in place.

If you prefer, use the diagram and instructions opposite to make your box.

Line the box with waxed paper, as suggested before, using dark paper for chocolates if possible. Then wrap every item singly, and arrange in rows in the box. Separate the rows with double thickness waxed paper and place a piece of card or waxed paper between layers. Don't make more than two layers or the bottom ones will be squashed.

When the box is filled, make it as airtight as possible. Fill any space between the sweets and the lid with padded or corrugated paper and close the lid carefully. Finish with ribbon and a gift card.

MAKE THEM LOOK LOVELY

LARGE RECTANGULAR BOX

1 Score dotted lines.
2 Stick tab A over flap A so that two sides form a corner. Do the same with tab B over flap B to make the sides and bottom of the box.
3 Stick tab C to side C, forming a box shape.
4 Fold inside parts D, E and F. This produces the self lining for the front, sides and bottom of the box.
5 Fold in the lid, with tongue, marked T, inside.

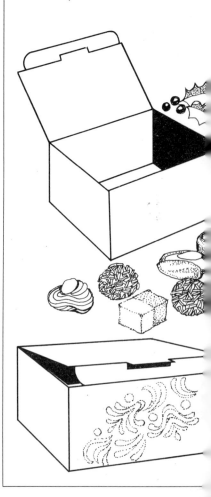

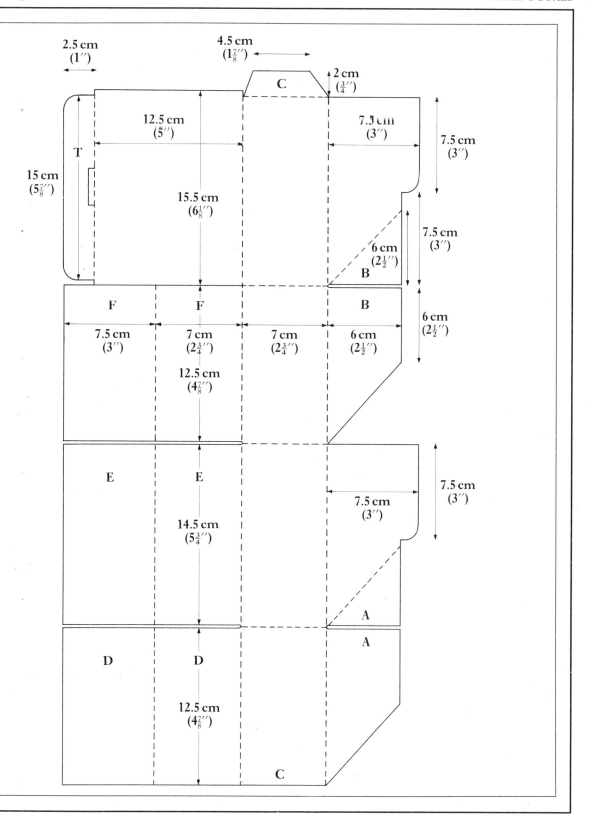

MIXED FRUIT MINCEMEAT

Makes about 2 kg (4½ lb)

125 g (4 oz) dried apricots

125 g (4 oz) dried figs

125 g (4 oz) cut mixed peel

225 g (8 oz) currants

225 g (8 oz) seedless raisins

225 g (8 oz) sultanas

225 g (8 oz) shredded suet

175 g (6 oz) chopped mixed nuts

450 g (1 lb) demerara sugar

30 ml (2 tbsp) orange marmalade

finely grated rind and juice of 1 medium orange

finely grated rind and juice of 1 lemon

45 ml (3 tbsp) rum

45 ml (3 tbsp) sherry

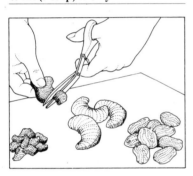

1 Snip the apricots and figs in small pieces into a large bowl. Add the remaining dry ingredients and mix together.

2 Stir in the marmalade with the finely grated orange and lemon rinds. Add the orange and lemon juices with the rum and sherry. (If the mincemeat is to be stored for more than 6 weeks, add an extra 45 ml (3 tbsp) each of rum and sherry.) Mix well.

3 Pack into warmed jars, cover and label. Store for at least 1 week before use.

CHERRY AND NUT MINCEMEAT

Makes about 1.5 kg (3 lb)

225 g (8 oz) glacé cherries

125 g (4 oz) shelled walnuts, chopped

175 g (6 oz) currants

175 g (6 oz) seedless raisins

175 g (6 oz) sultanas

225 g (8 oz) firm, hard cooking apples, such as Wellingtons, peeled, cored and grated

125 g (4 oz) shredded suet

350 g (12 oz) demerara sugar

5 ml (1 tsp) ground mixed spice

300 ml (½ pint) brandy or rum

1 Place all the ingredients in a large bowl. Mix well together, cover and leave for 2 days.

2 Stir well and put into warmed jars. Cover and label. Allow at least 2 weeks to mature before use.

CANDIED ORANGE PEEL

Makes about 225 g (8 oz)

6 oranges

350 g (12 oz) granulated sugar

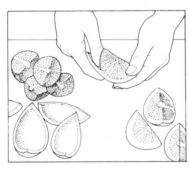

1 Wash or scrub the oranges thoroughly, halve or quarter them and remove the peel. Large pieces of peel retain their moisture better, so do not cut them up.

2 Simmer the peel in a little water for 1–2 hours, stirring occasionally, until tender.

3 Drain the liquid into a measuring jug and make up to 300 ml (½ pint) with water.

4 Pour the liquid into a clean pan, add 250 g (8 oz) of the sugar, dissolve over low heat, then bring to the boil. Add the peel, remove from the heat and leave in a cool place for 2 days.

5 Drain off the syrup again into a clean pan. Add the remaining sugar, dissolve over low heat, then add the peel and simmer until semi-transparent. The peel can be left in this thick syrup for 2–3 weeks.

6 Drain off the syrup and place the peel on a wire rack to dry. Put the rack in a warm place such as an airing cupboard. The temperature should not exceed 50°C (120°F) or the peel may brown and the flavour spoil.

7 The drying will take several hours and is completed when the peel is no longer sticky. When thoroughly dried, pack as described in box opposite. If liked, finish the peel with a glacé or crystallised finish (see opposite).

FINISHING THE CANDIED PEEL

If liked, give the peel one of the following finishes before packing.

Crystallised finish: Take the pieces of candied peel and dip each quickly into boiling water. Drain off excess moisture, then roll each piece in caster sugar.

Glacé finish: Prepare a fresh syrup, using 450 g (1 lb) sugar and 150 ml ($\frac{1}{4}$ pint) water, bring to the boil and boil for 1 minute. Pour a little of the syrup into a cup. Dip the candied peel into boiling water for 20 seconds, then dip them one at a time in the syrup, using a skewer. Place the peel on a wire rack to dry. Cover the rest of the syrup in the pan with a damp cloth and keep it warm (a double pan is useful for this purpose). As the syrup in the cup becomes cloudy, replace it with fresh. Dry the peel as before, turning it occasionally.

Using the surplus syrup: After the peel has been removed, the surplus syrup can be used in several different ways. It has a delicious fruity flavour and is the consistency of honey. Add to fruit salads and sauces or use to sweeten puddings or stewed fruit.

Packing the candied peel: Pack the peel in cardboard or wooden boxes, keeping each piece separate between layers of waxed paper. If preferred, store in jars covered with a piece of paper or cloth over the top. Containers must not be sealed or airtight as the peel may become mouldy under these conditions.

CARAMELLED FRUITS

about 450 g (1 lb) mixed prepared fresh fruits such as orange or mandarin segments, small pieces of pineapple, black or white grapes, cherries or strawberries
225 g (8 oz) preserving sugar
5 ml (1 tsp) powdered glucose
a large pinch of cream of tartar

1 Oil a marble slab or large plate. Wash and dry the fruit carefully, discarding any with bruises or defects. Skewer each piece of fruit on a fork or wooden cocktail stick.

2 Put the sugar in a small, deep, heavy-based saucepan with 60 ml (4 tbsp) water. Heat gently until the sugar has dissolved, then add the glucose and cream of tartar. Boil gently until it is golden brown and has reached a temperature of 143°C (290°F).

3 Dip the prepared fruit, one piece at a time, into the syrup. Drain well by tapping the fork or stick gently on the edge of the saucepan and place on the marble slab or plate.

4 Leave, without touching, until quite dry. Then place in paper cases. Serve as petits fours.

CRYSTALLISING

Most flowers are suitable, except those grown from bulbs as they are poisonous. The best results are obtained from flattish flowers with a small number of petals, eg violets, primroses, rose petals, fruit blossoms—apple, pear or cherry. Choose whole flowers that are fresh and free from damage, bruises or brown marks. Pick them in the morning once the dew has lifted and the petals are dry.

CRYSTALLISED FLOWERS, PETALS OR LEAVES

1 egg white
flowers, petals or leaves
caster sugar

1 Lightly whisk the egg white. Divide the flowers, petals or leaves, leaving a short piece of stalk if possible.

2 Paint both sides of each flower, petal or leaf with the lightly whisked egg white.

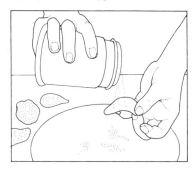

3 Sprinkle both sides with caster sugar, shaking off the excess. Leave to dry.

4 If necessary, sprinkle a second time with sugar to ensure they are evenly coated. Leave to dry completely before storing in an airtight container or screw-topped jar. Use to decorate cakes or desserts.

Basic Recipes

Turkey, plum pudding and Christmas cake are all very well, but the festive board doesn't groan until you add the stuffings, sauces and gravies, brandy butter for the mince pies and traditional relishes for the cold meats. Creative use of these accompaniments, plus imaginative vegetables and salads, will make your Christmas cooking truly memorable.

Vegetables and Salads

CHESTNUT AND SPROUT SAUTÉ

Serves 8

900 g (2 lb) fresh chestnuts or 879 g (1 lb 15 oz) can whole chestnuts

600 ml (1 pint) chicken stock

700 g (1½ lb) Brussels sprouts

salt and freshly ground pepper

450 g (1 lb) medium onions, skinned

225 g (8 oz) celery, trimmed

125 g (4 oz) butter

finely grated rind of 1 lemon

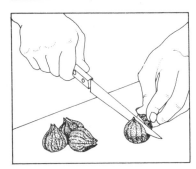

1 If using fresh chestnuts, snip the brown outer skins, or nick with a sharp knife. Place in boiling water for 3–5 minutes.

2 Lift the chestnuts out a few at a time, then peel off both the brown and inner skins. Put the nuts in a saucepan, cover with the stock and simmer for 40–45 minutes until tender. Drain well.

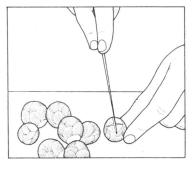

3 Meanwhile, trim the sprouts and pull off any damaged or discoloured outer leaves. With a sharp knife, make a cross in the stalk end of each one.

4 Cook the sprouts in boiling salted water for 3–4 minutes only; drain well.

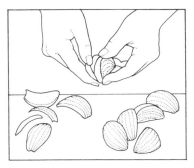

5 Quarter the onions and separate out the layers. Cut the celery into 2.5 cm (1 inch) pieces.

6 Melt the butter in a large sauté or frying pan. Add the onions and celery with the lemon rind and sauté for 2–3 minutes until softened. Add the cooked chestnuts, Brussels sprouts and salt and pepper to taste. Sauté for a further 1–2 minutes until heated through. Serve immediately.

PARSNIP AND CARROT AU GRATIN

Serves 4–6

450 g (1 lb) parsnips, peeled
450 g (1 lb) carrots, peeled
600 ml (1 pint) chicken stock
salt and freshly ground pepper
25 g (1 oz) butter
50 g (2 oz) fresh breadcrumbs
30 ml (2 tbsp) chopped fresh
   parsley, to garnish

1 Chop the parsnips and carrots coarsely and place in a saucepan with the stock and salt and pepper to taste. Bring to the boil, cover and simmer gently for 15–20 minutes until well cooked. Drain and cool slightly.

2 Purée the vegetables in a blender or rub through a sieve. Add the butter and turn into a flameproof dish. Sprinkle the breadcrumbs over the surface and cook under a hot grill until golden brown. Garnish with parsley and serve hot.

DIJON POTATOES

Serves 6

900 g (2 lb) potatoes, peeled
2 large onions, skinned
30 ml (2 tbsp) snipped chives
30 ml (2 tbsp) Dijon mustard
300 ml (½ pint) chicken stock
salt and freshly ground pepper
25 g (1 oz) butter

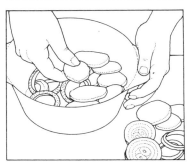

1 Slice the potatoes and onion thinly and arrange in alternate layers in a casserole dish. Sprinkle each layer with the chives and end with a potato layer.

2 Blend the mustard and stock together with salt and pepper to taste. Pour over the potatoes.

3 Melt the butter in a pan and brush over the top. Cover and bake in the oven at 180°C (350°F) mark 4 for 2 hours.

4 Remove the lid 30 minutes before the end of the cooking time to brown the top. Serve hot.

GOLDEN OVEN-FRIED POTATOES

Serves 6

1.1 kg (2½ lb) medium potatoes
   (about 6)
salt and freshly ground pepper
60 ml (4 tbsp) vegetable oil
25 g (1 oz) butter

1 Peel the potatoes, place in a large saucepan and cover with cold water. Add a good pinch of salt and bring to the boil. Cover and simmer for 8–10 minutes only, then drain.

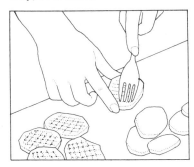

2 Cut the potatoes into 0.5–1 cm (¼–½ inch) slices and score the surfaces in both directions with a sharp-pronged fork.

3 Heat the oil and butter in a roasting tin measuring about 30.5 × 23 cm (12 × 9 inches). Add the potato slices, turn them over in the fat, then sprinkle with salt and pepper to taste.

4 Bake the potatoes in the oven at 200°C (400°F) mark 6 for about 1¼ hours, turning once. Drain off the fat before serving.

POTATO AND CARROT RÖSTI

Serves 2

450 g (1 lb) even-sized potatoes
salt and freshly ground pepper
175 g (6 oz) carrots, peeled
15 ml (1 tbsp) snipped chives
50 g (2 oz) butter or margarine

1 Scrub the potatoes and place in a large saucepan. Cover with cold water, add a good pinch of salt and bring to the boil. Cover and simmer for 7 minutes only.

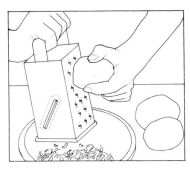

2 Drain the potatoes well, remove the skins and grate the flesh into a bowl.

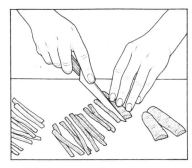

3 Cut the carrots lengthways, into fine, stumpy matchsticks. Blanch in boiling salted water for 5 minutes. Drain well.

4 Combine the carrots with the potato, chives and plenty of salt and pepper.

5 Melt the butter in a frying pan, add the potato mixture and form into a 15 cm (6 inch) cake. Fry for 7 minutes a side.

RED CABBAGE AND BEETROOT SALAD

Serves 6

275 g (10 oz) red cabbage, trimmed and very finely shredded

225 g (8 oz) cooked beetroot, skinned and diced

1 small onion, skinned and finely chopped

30 ml (2 tbsp) vegetable oil

15–30 ml (1–2 tbsp) red wine vinegar

salt and freshly ground pepper

1 Put the cabbage, beetroot and onion in a salad bowl and toss until well mixed.

2 In a screw-topped jar or bowl, shake or whisk together the oil, vinegar and salt and freshly ground pepper to taste.

3 Add the dressing to the bowl and lightly toss again. Leave for 30 minutes before serving.

LEEK AND SPROUT SALAD

Serves 4

225 g (8 oz) fresh Brussels sprouts, trimmed

175 g (6 oz) leeks

30 ml (2 tbsp) vegetable oil

30 ml (2 tbsp) distilled vinegar

5 ml (1 tsp) celery seeds

salt and freshly ground pepper

1 Slice the sprouts very thinly. Place in a salad bowl.

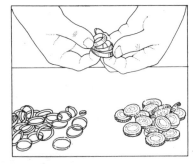

2 Slice the leeks thinly. Wash thoroughly, drain, then separate into rings.

3 Place the leeks in boiling water for 1–2 minutes. Drain and pat dry. Add to the sprouts.

4 In a screw-topped jar or bowl, shake or whisk together the oil, vinegar, celery seeds and salt and pepper to taste.

5 Add the dressing to the bowl and toss well to mix with the vegetables. Chill in the refrigerator for about 30 minutes before serving.

STUFFINGS

LIVER AND BACON STUFFING

Sufficient to fill the neck end of a 4.4–5.4 kg (10–12 lb) oven ready turkey.

125 g (4 oz) turkey liver—from the turkey

225 g (8 oz) streaky bacon, rinded and finely chopped

1 medium onion, skinned and finely chopped

50 g (2 oz) butter or margarine

225 g (8 oz) fresh breadcrumbs

30 ml (2 tbsp) chopped fresh parsley

salt and freshly ground pepper

1 egg, beaten

1 Wash the liver, remove any fat and chop roughly. Combine with the bacon and onion.

2 Melt the butter in a frying pan, add the liver, bacon and onion and fry over brisk heat for 5 minutes.

3 Put the breadcrumbs in a bowl with the parsley. Add the liver and bacon mixture and plenty of salt and pepper. Mix well.

4 Bind the mixture with the beaten egg and knead together with the fingertips. Leave until cold before using for stuffing poultry.

MINT AND ROSEMARY STUFFING

Sufficient to fill the neck end of a 4.4–5.4 kg (10–12 lb) oven ready turkey.

75 g (3 oz) butter or margarine

2 medium onions, skinned and finely chopped

2 celery sticks, trimmed and finely chopped

225 g (8 oz) fresh breadcrumbs

30 ml (2 tbsp) mint sauce

10 ml (2 tsp) dried rosemary

finely grated rind of 1 lemon

salt and freshly ground pepper

1 egg, beaten

1 Melt the butter in a frying pan, add the onions and celery and fry gently for about 10 minutes.

2 Place the breadcrumbs, mint sauce, rosemary and lemon rind in a bowl. Mix well together. Stir in the celery and onion and plenty of salt and pepper.

3 Bind the mixture with the beaten egg and knead together with the fingertips. Leave until cold before using for stuffing poultry.

PRUNE, APPLE AND CELERY STUFFING

Makes about 700 g (1½ lb)

12 prunes

150 ml (¼ pint) port

50 g (2 oz) butter or margarine

2 large onions, skinned and finely chopped

1 medium celery head, trimmed and finely chopped

2 large cooking apples, peeled, cored and chopped

salt and freshly ground pepper

1 Put the prunes in a bowl, pour over the port, cover and leave to soak for 12 hours.

2 Melt the butter in a frying pan, add the onions and celery and fry gently until just softened.

3 Meanwhile, drain the prunes, reserving the soaking liquid. Stone the prunes; chop roughly.

4 Add the prunes and their soaking liquid to the frying pan with the chopped apple. Add plenty of salt and pepper and cook, stirring, for 1 minute. Leave until cold before using.

SAGE AND ONION STUFFING

Makes about 800 g (1¾ lb)

50 g (2 oz) butter or margarine
450 g (1 lb) onions, skinned and finely chopped
10 ml (2 tsp) dried sage
225 g (8 oz) fresh breadcrumbs
125 g (4 oz) medium oatmeal
salt and freshly ground pepper

1 Melt the butter in a frying pan, add the onions and sage and fry gently for 4–5 minutes. Stir in the breadcrumbs.

2 Toast the oatmeal under the grill. Stir into the breadcrumb mixture with plenty of salt and pepper. Leave until cold before using for stuffing poultry or pork.

SAUCES AND RELISHES

GIBLET GRAVY

Makes 600 ml (1 pint)

poultry giblets
1 small onion
1 small carrot, peeled
1 celery stick, trimmed and chopped
bacon rinds
salt and freshly ground pepper
15 ml (1 tbsp) plain flour
butter

1 Put the gizzard, heart and neck (not the liver) in a saucepan with the vegetables, a few bacon rinds, 1.1 litres (2 pints) water and salt and pepper. Bring to the boil, cover and simmer for 2 hours.

2 Strain the giblet stock into a basin. Discard the vegetables and bacon rinds and, if you wish, set aside the cooked giblets for use in another dish.

3 When cooked, remove the bird to a warm plate and pour off most of the fat from the tin, leaving behind the sediment and about 30 ml (2 tbsp) fat.

4 Blend the flour into the fat in the roasting tin. Cook until it turns brown, stirring continuously and scraping any sediment from the bottom of the tin. Slowly stir in 600 ml (1 pint) giblet stock. Bring to the boil, stirring.

5 Meanwhile, sauté the liver in a knob of butter until just cooked. Remove from the pan, drain and chop it into small pieces.

6 Add the chopped liver to the gravy and simmer for 2–3 minutes to heat. Check the seasoning. Pour into a gravy boat or jug and keep hot until needed.

CRANBERRY AND APPLE JELLY

1.4 kg (3 lb) cooking apples, washed
900 g (2 lb) cranberries, washed
sugar

1 Remove any bruised or damaged portions from the apples, then chop them roughly without peeling or coring.

2 Put the apples and cranberries in a preserving pan with sufficient water to cover and simmer gently for 45 minutes– 1 hour until the fruit is really soft and pulpy. Stir from time to time to prevent sticking.

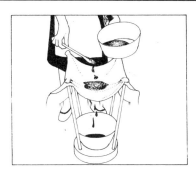

3 Spoon the pulp into a jelly bag or cloth attached to the legs of an upturned stool. Strain into a bowl for at least 12 hours.

4 Discard the pulp remaining in the jelly bag. Measure the extract and return it to the pan with 450 g (1 lb) sugar for each 600 ml (1 pint) extract. Heat gently, stirring, until the sugar has dissolved, then boil rapidly for about 10 minutes until a temperature of 105°C (221°F) registers on a sugar thermometer.

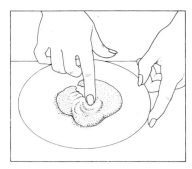

5 If you do not have a sugar thermometer, test for a set by spooning a little jelly on to a chilled saucer. Leave to cool, then push a finger across the surface. When setting point has been reached, the surface will wrinkle.

6 Remove the pan from the heat and remove any scum with a slotted spoon.

7 Pour the jelly into preheated jars. Place a disc of waxed paper across the surface of the jelly, cover the jar with dampened Cellophane and secure with an elastic band. Serve with turkey.

HORSERADISH SAUCE

Serves 4

30 ml (2 tbsp) finely grated horseradish
10 ml (2 tsp) caster sugar
1.25 ml ($\frac{1}{4}$ tsp) prepared mustard
15 ml (1 tbsp) white wine vinegar
salt and freshly ground pepper
150 ml ($\frac{1}{4}$ pint) double cream

1 Mix together the horseradish, sugar, mustard, vinegar and salt and pepper to taste.

2 Whip the cream lightly, then gradually stir into the mixture. Serve chilled with roast beef.

BREAD SAUCE

Serves 6

2 cloves
1 medium onion, skinned
1 small bay leaf
450 ml ($\frac{3}{4}$ pint) milk
75 g (3 oz) fresh white breadcrumbs
salt and white pepper
15 g ($\frac{1}{2}$ oz) butter
30 ml (2 tbsp) single cream

1 Stick the cloves into the onion and place in a small heavy-based pan with the bay leaf and milk to cover.

2 Bring slowly to the boil, remove from the heat, cover and leave to infuse for 10 minutes.

3 Remove the onion and bay leaf, then add the bread-crumbs and salt and pepper to taste. Return to the heat and simmer gently for 10–15 minutes, stirring occasionally. Stir in the butter and cream. Serve with roast turkey, chicken or pheasant.

CHESTNUT SAUCE

Serves 4

225 g (8 oz) chestnuts
300 ml ($\frac{1}{2}$ pint) chicken stock
1 small piece of onion, skinned
1 small piece of carrot, peeled
40 g ($1\frac{1}{2}$ oz) butter
45 ml (3 tbsp) plain flour
salt and freshly ground pepper
30–45 ml (2–3 tbsp) single cream

1 Snip the brown outer skins of the chestnuts. Place in boiling water for 3–5 minutes. Lift out, a few at a time, and peel off both the brown and inner skins.

2 Put the peeled nuts in a sauce-pan with the stock and vegetables. Cover and simmer for about 45 minutes until soft, then mash or sieve to a purée.

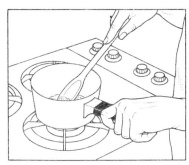

3 Melt the butter in a clean saucepan, add the flour and cook gently, stirring, for 1–2 minutes. Add the chestnut purée and bring to the boil, stirring. The sauce should be thick, but it may be necessary at this point to add a little milk or extra stock.

4 Season well with salt and pepper, remove from the heat and stir in the cream. Reheat without boiling. Serve with turkey or other poultry.

ORANGE AND APPLE CHUTNEY

Makes about 2.3 kg (5 lb)

1.8 kg (4 lb) cooking apples
450 g (1 lb) stoned raisins
2 oranges
700 ml ($1\frac{1}{4}$ pints) malt vinegar
900 g (2 lb) granulated sugar

1 Peel, quarter, core and roughly chop the apples. Finely chop the raisins.

2 Pare the orange rind using a potato peeler, then chop finely. Squeeze the orange juice.

3 Cook the apples, raisins and peel with 500 ml (1 pint) of the vinegar in a covered pan until the apples are soft.

4 Add the sugar, remaining vinegar and orange juice. Stir to dissolve.

5 Cook gently, uncovered, stirring frequently until the chutney is thick, well reduced and no excess liquid remains.

6 Pour into preheated jars and cover with airtight, vinegar-proof tops. Store for 1 month to mature before eating.

BEETROOT CHUTNEY

Makes about 3.6 kg (8 lb)

1.4 kg (3 lb) raw beetroot, peeled and grated
900 g (2 lb) cooking apples, peeled, cored and chopped
450 g (1 lb) onions, skinned and chopped
450 g (1 lb) seedless raisins
1.4 litres ($2\frac{1}{2}$ pints) malt vinegar
1.1 kg ($2\frac{1}{2}$ lb) granulated sugar
30 ml (2 tbsp) ground ginger
juice of 1 lemon

1 Place all the ingredients in a preserving pan and bring to the boil.

2 Simmer gently, uncovered, stirring occasionally, for about $2\frac{1}{2}$ hours, until no excess liquid remains and the mixture is thick.

3 Spoon the chutney into pre-heated jars and cover immediately with airtight, vinegar-proof tops. Store for 1 month to mature before eating.

BRANDY BUTTER

Serves 6–8

100 g (4 oz) butter, softened
100 g (4 oz) icing sugar, sifted
100 g (4 oz) caster sugar
15 ml (1 tbsp) milk
15 ml (1 tbsp) brandy

1 Beat the butter in a bowl until pale and light. Gradually beat in the icing and caster sugars, alternately with the milk and brandy. Beat until light and fluffy.

2 Pile into a small dish and leave to harden before serving. Serve with Christmas pudding.

RUM BUTTER

1 Follow the recipe for Brandy Butter, but use soft brown sugar instead of the icing and caster sugars, and replace the brandy by 45 ml (3 tbsp) rum.

2 Add the finely grated rind of half a lemon and a squeeze of lemon juice.

SWEET WHITE SAUCE

Makes 300 ml ($\frac{1}{2}$ pint)

20 g ($\frac{3}{4}$ oz) butter
30 ml (2 tbsp) plain flour
300 ml ($\frac{1}{2}$ pint) milk
25 ml ($1\frac{1}{2}$ tbsp) caster sugar

1 Melt the butter in a saucepan, add the flour and cook gently, stirring, for 1–2 minutes. Remove from the heat and gradually blend in the milk.

2 Bring to the boil, stirring constantly, then simmer for 3 minutes until thick and smooth. Add the sugar to taste.

EGG CUSTARD

Makes 300 ml ($\frac{1}{2}$ pint)

2 eggs
10 ml (2 tsp) caster sugar
300 ml ($\frac{1}{2}$ pint) milk
5 ml (1 tsp) vanilla flavouring (optional)

1 Beat the eggs in a bowl with the sugar and 45 ml (3 tbsp) of the milk. Heat the rest of the milk in a saucepan to lukewarm, then beat into the eggs.

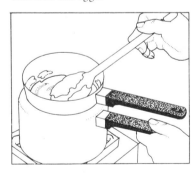

2 Pour into a double saucepan or bowl standing over a pan of simmering water. Cook, stirring continuously, until the custard thickens enough to thinly coat the back of the spoon. Do not boil.

3 Pour into a cold jug and stir in the vanilla flavouring, if using. Serve hot or cold. The sauce thickens slightly on cooling.

DRESSINGS

MAYONNAISE

Makes 150 ml ($\frac{1}{4}$ pint)

1 egg yolk
5 ml (1 tsp) Dijon mustard
2.5 ml ($\frac{1}{2}$ tsp) salt
1.25 ml ($\frac{1}{4}$ tsp) freshly ground pepper
2.5 ml ($\frac{1}{2}$ tsp) sugar
15 ml (1 tbsp) white wine or cider vinegar or lemon juice
about 150 ml ($\frac{1}{4}$ pint) sunflower oil

1 Put the egg yolk into a bowl with the mustard, seasoning, sugar and 5 ml (1 tsp) of the vinegar or lemon juice.

2 Mix thoroughly, then add the oil, *drop by drop*, stirring briskly with a wooden spoon the whole time, or whisking until sauce is thick.

3 Add a little more vinegar or lemon juice if sauce is too thick. When all the oil has been added, add the remaining vinegar or lemon juice gradually and mix thoroughly.

VINAIGRETTE

(FRENCH DRESSING)

Makes 135 ml (9 tbsp)

90 ml (6 tbsp) olive oil
45 ml (3 tbsp) white wine or cider vinegar or lemon juice
2.5 ml ($\frac{1}{2}$ tsp) sugar
2.5 ml ($\frac{1}{2}$ tsp) wholegrain, Dijon or French mustard
salt and freshly ground pepper

1 Place all the ingredients in a bowl or screw-topped jar and whisk or shake together.

2 Before use, whisk or shake the dressing again, as otherwise the oil separates out on standing.

PASTRIES AND SAVOURIES

SHORTCRUST PASTRY

For shortcrust pastry, use half the quantity of fat to flour. Therefore, for a recipe using quantities of shortcrust pastry other than 225 g (8 oz) simply use half the quantity of fat to flour weight specified.

225 g (8 oz) plain flour

pinch of salt

50 g (2 oz) butter or block margarine

50 g (2 oz) lard

1 Sift the flour and salt together in a bowl. Cut the butter and lard into small pieces and add to the flour.

2 Lightly rub in the butter or margarine and the lard with your fingertips until the mixture resembles fine breadcrumbs.

3 Add 30–45 ml (2–3 tbsp) chilled water evenly over the surface and stir in until the mixture begins to stick together in large lumps.

4 With one hand, collect the mixture together to form a ball. Knead lightly for a few seconds to give a firm, smooth dough. Do not over-handle.

5 The pastry can be used straightaway, but it is better if allowed to 'rest' for about 30 minutes wrapped in foil in the refrigerator.

6 Roll out the pastry on a lightly floured surface to a thickness about 3 mm ($\frac{1}{8}$ inch). Do not pull or stretch the pastry. To cook, the usual oven temperature for shortcrust pastry is 200°–220°C (400°–425°F) mark 6–7.

ACCOMPANIMENTS TO POULTRY

Bacon Rolls

Remove the rind from rashers of streaky bacon and then neatly roll up the rashers.

Thread the rolls on skewers, put in the roasting tin and cook in the oven with the roast poultry for about the last 30 minutes of the cooking time.

Chipolatas

Twist chipolata sausages in half and cut each of them into two; 225 g (8 oz) chipolatas makes sixteen. Put in a single layer in a baking tin and cook in the oven with the roast poultry for about the last 30 minutes of the cooking time until golden. To keep hot, cover the tin with foil and keep in a warm place. Drain on absorbent kitchen paper before serving.

SAUSAGE ROLLS

Makes 16

175 g (6 oz) shortcrust pastry, made with 175 g (6 oz) flour (see left)

225 g (8 oz) pork sausagemeat

flour, for dredging

a little milk

beaten egg, to glaze

1 On a lightly floured surface, roll out the pastry thinly to an oblong, then cut it lengthways into 2 strips. Divide the sausagemeat into 2 pieces, dust with flour, and form into 2 rolls the same length of the pastry.

2 Lay a roll of sausagemeat down the centre of each strip, brush the edges of the pastry with a little milk, fold one side of the pastry over the sausagemeat and press the two edges firmly together. Seal the long edges.

3 Brush the length of the two rolls with egg, then cut each into slices 4–5 cm (1$\frac{1}{2}$–2 inches) long. Place on a baking sheet and bake in the oven at 200°C (400°F) mark 6 for 15 minutes. Reduce the temperature to 180°C (350°F) mark 4 and cook for a further 15 minutes. Serve hot or cold.

FLAN PASTRY

100 g (4 oz) plain flour

pinch of salt

75 g (3 oz) butter or block margarine and lard

5 ml (1 tsp) caster sugar

1 egg, beaten

1 Mix the flour and salt together in a bowl. Cut the fat into small pieces and add it to the flour.

2 Rub in the fat until the mixture resembles fine breadcrumbs. Stir in the sugar.

3 Add the egg, stirring with a round-bladed knife until the ingredients begin to stick together in large lumps.

4 With one hand, collect the mixture together and knead lightly for a few seconds to give a firm, smooth dough.

5 Roll out as for shortcrust pastry; use as required. When cooking flan pastry, the usual oven temperature is 200°C (400°F) mark 6.

INDEX